GET THE MONKEYS OFF YOUR BACK

*How to be confident, fearless and tough
in school and in life*

DANIEL MERZA

First published by Busybird Publishing 2018
Copyright © 2018 Daniel Merza

ISBN
Print: 978-1-925692-64-8
Ebook: 978-1-925692-65-5

Cover design: Busybird Publishing
Illustrator: Michael Arvithis
Layout and typesetting: Busybird Publishing
Editor: Robert Frolla

Busybird Publishing
2/118 Para Road
Montmorency, Victoria
Australia 3094
www.busybird.com.au

DANIEL MERZA
EDUCATE · EMPOWER · INSPIRE

ENDORSEMENTS

Daniel Merza is both a bold and brave new voice in providing young people with the emotional literacy to identify the 'monkeys on their back' and to challenge the status quo which limits their potential.

Written with a uniquely distinctive voice, whilst drawing upon the wisdom of the ages, Daniel is able to communicate directly with young people to explore the challenges of contemporary adolescence and emerging adulthood. It is authentic in that Daniel draws upon his own experience and written with a lightness in tone to deflect the serious nature of much of the conversation.

I would heartily recommend this book as an enlightening read for adults, educators and young people seeking to discover the best version of themselves. Daniel's commitment to ensure that young people engage with life, fully aware of the various pressures and challenges, they will confront both internally and externally is commendable. His own purpose is clear!

Dr Steven Middleton, Head of Berwick Grammar School

In his book *Get the Monkeys off Your Back*, Daniel Merza, an accomplished motivational speaker, draws on personal experiences as an adolescent to provide insight into what holds young people back. As a principal in a Positive Education school, his message spoke to me and will touch the lives of young people, parents and educators alike. His personal accounts of being bullied give this highly readable and accessible work true credibility. Written from the heart, as a young man who experienced the effects of bullying, his brutal honesty is inspiring and his practical exercises will give young people from all walks of life relatable scenarios and strategies to move from 'victim to victor'.

A compelling read.

Peter Wade, Principal, Patrician Brothers' College, Fairfield

Daniel Merza has written from the heart.

As a high school teacher with many years of experience and as a mother of two teenagers, reading this book gave me many new ideas in how to manage the various curved balls that life throws at our kids these days. Especially the newer problems, such as cyber bullying and internet addiction.

Every chapter is packed with stories from real life and each one suggests practical, well-balanced thoughts on how to cope with these challenges. It is written in simple, easy-to-read language that teens can relate to and understand, and the exercises at the end of each chapter are encouraging and supportive.

I think I even built a little more 'emotional muscle', as Daniel calls it, myself!

Rita Fin, Assistant to the Headmaster, Sydney Grammar School

Daniel has provided an inspirational, practical resource for teens to see the light in any situation, build resilience, develop self-awareness and 'get the monkeys off their back,' so they can truly thrive. It's modern, readable and the personal stories make it real and provide *hope* for any teen facing challenges. There's also an underlying message of compassion and understanding towards others by reading the trials and tribulations of a diverse group of people. This is an important book for any teen.

Amanda Rootsey, Youth Mentor, Author and Founder of Teen Academy, 'Shine From Within'

Daniel Merza's book – *Get the Monkeys off Your Back* – is an exciting one. Filled with real life stories, from himself and others he has interviewed, this book is emotional, raw, relevant, and most of all, it is practical. With summaries at the end of each chapter and practical application exercises, so it won't just be another nice book you read, it will be something that you can apply to your life – to change your life, literally! Young people need to read this, as should older people. Bravo Daniel, a brilliant book that will impact the next generation.

Brett Murray, CEO, Co-founder of the Make Bullying History Foundation, Author, Professional Speaker

This is a wonderful and easy-to-understand book which thoughtfully draws on the many challenges and sources of anxiety in young people today and unpacks effective ways to deal with them. I found the clear and concise format of topic, exercise and summary makes this book a fantastic source for students to re-read in times they are feeling most in need for some support. Rhetorical questions throughout the book allow young readers to engage with the written text simply, allowing them to adapt the examples to their own life. A *must-read* for all teenagers.

Year 12 Student

Get the Monkeys off Your Back is a must-read book for anyone interested in leveling out the peaks and troughs of their adolescent journey of self-discovery.

We are told that resilience is the key to survive and thrive, but are not often given the tools required to nurture or develop resilience. Daniel Merza's monkey metaphor is a quirky and appealing one, which will appeal to his teen target audience and keep them engaged as he imparts his wisdom to educate and empower them. These monkeys, which have personalities and names, represent common limiting beliefs, allowing the reader to easily identify which of the limiting beliefs, or 'monkeys' are holding them back. The five monkeys, together with the exercises at the conclusion of each chapter, provide a useful tool kit to help develop the resilience required to navigate life and provide a guide towards the achievement of the reader's full potential.

Randa Habelrih, Multi-international Award-winning Speaker, Author and Social Inclusion Advocate

Goosebumps! Awesome! This is a fantastic book with a truly inspiring and heartfelt message, and features a truly remarkable series of stories and practical tips on how to overcome challenges and become a better version of yourself. I love how the book focuses on emotional resilience and mental wellbeing, and also how it has the ability to help the reader develop confidence and self-belief. I hope every young person has the opportunity to read this book.

Marco Capobianco, CEO, Conviction Group

Navigating the minefield of adolescence has never been more challenging. As such, a book like Daniel's is such a valuable tool for giving young people the tools, insights and inspiration to thrive in the all-important final years of school life.

Michael McQueen, CSP, Five-time Bestselling Author and Youth Trends Expert

As a teacher and parent, I believe that Daniel has written a very important and beneficial book that will guide students during their difficult teenage years. It will allow students to tackle their studies, especially Year 12, and be armed with practical strategies in building up their resilience and working to the best of their ability. I was moved and inspired by the case studies provided and particularly by Daniel's strategies. I wholeheartedly endorse his advice and guidance.

Marella Healy, High School Teacher, Parent

Youthful, dynamic and engaging from start to finish. Our boys took away a great deal from Daniel's presentation on resilience and achieving their personal best. Daniel's passion was evident as he instilled in the boys the importance of making the most of their short block of time remaining at school by adopting a strong work ethic, to be true to oneself, and to be perseverant. We'll definitely have Daniel back again.

Michael Webb, Year 10 Boarding Master, St Ignatius' College, Riverview

Daniel gives a simple and practical guide to help improve both your mentality and spirituality towards achieving or accomplishing anything. Coming from a background which meant that marks were the only means of success, the book shows and reassures you that there are actually so many ways to achieve victory. Everyone goes through a tough time and this book gives a strong encouragement to help you persevere and stay determined on the road ahead in any given circumstance.

Year 12 Student

DEDICATION

To Mum and Dad, *Ayoub* and *Ghada Merza* – your love is like no other, so special that there never has or ever will be anything that can replace this love. You've always had my back and I know you always will.

There would be no book without your unconditional love, support and guidance throughout my life. You both mean the world to me and have shaped me into the man I am today. Thank you.

In honour and memory of *Gabriella Wehbe* (7.10.1998 – 9.3.2018), for being the true definition of resilience and inspiring me on my journey. You will never be forgotten.

.

Contents

ACKNOWLEDGMENTS

F irstly, and above all, I'd like to praise *God*, The Father, Son and Holy Spirit for standing with me always and filling my life with amazing grace, abundant blessings and unstoppable love.

In addition to my loving parents, I would like to acknowledge and thank individual members of my family.

To my oldest sister, *Diane*, thank you for your endless offerings of advice and guidance, especially when transitioning from teen years to adulthood. My brother-in-law, *Nidal*, thank you for being a great role model and older brother to me, and for your continual encouraging words of wisdom.

To my sister *Mary*, a special thanks to you for always supporting me on my journey and my vision from the onset, and for being a sounding board throughout the writing process, even at the most inconvenient hours of the night. Your selflessness, authenticity, beauty and love has been a blessing.

To my brother *Georges* and sister-in-law *Casey*, thank you for generously sharing your creative ideas for the book design, and for your ongoing support throughout.

To my nephews, *Matthew, Joshua, Elijah* and *Isaiah*, thank you for bringing a bundle of joy to my life. May this work be my gift to you.

To my *circle of friends*, you've taught me so much about the definition of true friendship. Thank you for being able to count on you always.

To all the people *who have mentored me* over the years in my professional and business endeavours, thank you.

Thank you to *all interviewees* for giving up your time to openly share your personal stories for inclusion in this book. You have all inspired me immensely and I have learned so much from this experience. Thank you for being champion human beings and for your support throughout.

Thank you to *Natasa* and *Stuart Denman*, as well as *Blaise, Kev, Les and the Busybird Publishing team* for your guidance, patience and support through this first-time publishing experience.

To the super talented *Michael Arvithis*, my illustrator, thank you for your amazing creative work. Your illustrations truly added another dimension to this book.

A special thanks go to my former teacher and good friend *Anthony Chidiac*, for your guidance and encouragement every step of the way, including taking the time to read the manuscript and writing the foreword. Your feedback has been invaluable.

A big thank you to *Guy Zangari* for writing the foreword, sharing your experience and perspective, and for advocating the importance of this work.

To *all endorsers*: thank you for believing in me and my vision and for taking the time out to read the manuscript and being advocates of this work.

ACKNOWLEDGMENTS

To all the *schools, companies and communities* that I've spoken to, thank you for the opportunity and entrusting me to educate, empower and inspire. It's an honour and a privilege every time, and is something I don't take lightly.

To all past *bullies and naysayers*, thank you so much for being the foundation in which I built my resilience and shaping me into the person I am today. I wouldn't have it any other way.

Finally, to the *readers*, thank you for taking the time to read this book and embarking upon your path to becoming confident, fearless, and tough in school and in life, and allowing me the opportunity to open your hearts and minds to a future of endless possibilities.

FOREWORD

R esilience is a key factor in building personal character to achieve success in life following adverse situations. Life's journey throws challenges, twists and turns at individuals, and it's our response to these that determines how progress is made.

Young people are faced with a lot more scrutiny as a result of the ever-changing nature of technology and social media, which brings with it added pressures and expectations. Having worked with many families and students in my extensive career in Pastoral Care, Daniel's words of inspiration to overcome these hurdles and build resilience to reach their full potential are pivotal at this stage of their lives.

Shoulders to lean on, lived experiences and an empathetic ear are also critical to give an individual in despair the hope to push on and achieve goals. Daniel Merza has had his fair share of knocks in life. I can attest to this having witnessed him develop into a fine young man during my teaching career at Patrician Brothers' College Fairfield, Daniel's former high school.

Society needs more people like Daniel who are caring and sensitive to those needing a gentle helping hand. I congratulate Daniel on the publication of this book *Get the Monkeys off Your Back* and trust this will offer people ideas and strategies on how to overcome adversity.

Guy Zangari, MP

State Member for Fairfield

T he great Socrates challenges us 'to know ourselves.' This wisdom from ancient times is more relevant today than ever before. However, this sound advice is often difficult to practise. For some of us, it may take a lifetime to know who we really are and what our strengths and weaknesses are. This is when it becomes particularly necessary to seek the collective insights of others who have experienced life's challenges. In a sense, we need to 'stand on the shoulders of giants' to see things with the right clarity and perspective.

Daniel Merza is one such 'giant' who has gathered fascinating principles from personal experience and thorough research to help teenagers navigate their way around an increasingly complex and challenging world. I am confident these principles will help the young to make good decisions that will provide them with a solid platform in which to build a happy and successful life.

Get the Monkeys off Your Back is an excellent read. I found that it captures the issues facing teenagers today in a nutshell and provides an effective road map of how to deal with them. Often from my experience, the greatest obstacle is getting teenagers to firstly recognise that a problem exists, and this requires a great deal of honesty and humility. Once this is done, goals can be set and then followed by hard work under the guidance of mentors, so as to conquer these difficulties.

Daniel openly shares his personal story, outlining how he struggled to understand his path in life and how he picked himself up to go on to lead a more fulfilling life. Daniel doesn't just stop there; he cleverly threads together authentic and inspiring stories from a variety of rich sources. These courageous experiences really bring the book to life, making it relevant, meaningful and easy to relate to.

Overall, *Get the Monkeys off Your Back* is a wonderful achievement from such a young and up-and-coming writer. I welcome his deep passion to make a difference in the world by targeting the needs of the young. I too share his passion as I believe the young have the talent, vitality and energy that will sustain us in the future. I congratulate him on this book and am looking forward to his next exciting project.

Anthony Chidiac
Diverse Learning Teacher, Author,
Adolescent Counsellor and Parent

INTRODUCTION

In the midst of self-discovery, social survival and navigating life's possibilities on the rollercoaster adolescent journey, challenges will be faced along the way that can either make or break teens.

The call to be resilient has never been so loud.

Resilience is not a natural born ability. It is built.

With the added pressures of social media, research shows that many teens are struggling to cope with school and life challenges. Mental health issues, such as anxiety and eating disorders, addiction and depression, have become more common, and the incidents of bullying, self-harm, and suicide have increased. It doesn't have to be this way.

I know how difficult the teen years can be, having experienced barriers, challenges and insecurities of my own – personal, academic and social – that are not unique to me. Others have experienced challenges far greater in severity and hardship than mine.

I also know that no matter how hard life may be, or how hard life may get, it's possible to prevail over the hurdles, obstacles and trials, even when they seem to be insurmountable. I discovered this firsthand from personal experience, and through learning about the inspirational journey of others that I've personally interviewed from around the world. With consent, I have included these inspirational stories that demonstrate resilience from individuals of different backgrounds and experiences, who faced specific challenges during their teen years and overcame them to create prosperous futures. While some names have been changed for privacy reasons, the authenticity of their stories remains.

This book will educate, empower and inspire teens to break through barriers and show them how to build their resilience to overcome challenges and live up to their full potential. It addresses the most common challenges teens face. It's about character development, and is filled with strategies to empower readers to take control of their life and build the heart of resilience – the emotional muscle.

While targeted at teens (15–18 years old), readers of all ages and stages in life will greatly benefit, as the areas covered are not exclusive to teens.

This book is not a textbook. It aims to provide real life stories, analogies and examples to engage, inspire and convey key messages. The content shared is backed up by research and timeless principles.

It's a platform for reflection and will challenge readers and their perspective on life. Readers may find it confronting at times, especially when challenged to re-evaluate the status quo.

The book is best read in chronological order to ensure messages in later chapters are understood based on what was shared earlier in the book.

So it is recommended that all exercises are completed in a state of deep reflection while reading the book, including note-taking in a separate file where there is plenty of room to write.

And a final note to all readers: sharing this book is an immense honour, responsibility and pursuit that truly sets my heart on fire.

May this work be the catalyst that makes and shapes you into a resilient person in the future. May it empower you with strength to use life's challenges as opportunities to grow. May it ignite the light of hope to believe and achieve all that your heart desires.

Finally, may the following words always ring loud in the depths of your soul:

"Our deepest fear is not that we are inadequate. Our deepest fear is that we are powerful beyond measure."
— Marianne Williamson

Daniel Merza

1. TUNING IN

"I trust that everything happens for a reason, even if
we are not wise enough to see it."
– Oprah

When I recall my earliest memory of primary school, I hear the voices saying "Hey Monkey… Monkey Merza… ooo ooo aaa aaa!", a nickname given to me in Year 2 for trying to climb a tree. I was only seven. These early experiences planted a seed in me, and it grew for me to become a target for teasing.

From Year 2 to Year 4, it was mostly name calling and being made fun of. In Years 5 and 6, teasing turned into constant rejection, taunting and mocking. Hassled and harassed physically and regularly, I was getting into fights almost every day just trying to defend myself.

In the early years of high school, the verbal and physical bullying continued and they were really tough years – where I was socially rejected, emotionally unstable and academically disconnected. I needed help so sessions were arranged with the school counsellor first. When things were not improving, I was referred by my local doctor to see a psychiatrist. At thirteen, I was diagnosed with a mental illness and placed on medication for quite some time.

I experienced constant anxiety because I struggled to fit in and feel acceptance from both peers and teachers. I felt inadequate and struggled to accept myself, always feeling there was something wrong with me.

On many occasions, I received taunts that were damaging to my self-esteem, such as "You've got no hope", "You won't make it to Year 10" and "You're not going to make anything out of your life." It was a matter of survival at that point in my life.

By Year 10, I became a people-pleaser to gain social approval and fit in with the 'cool' group. It worked. That year, I became friends with Adrian and Pedro. We were always together at social outings – movies, birthday parties, and just hanging out. We would spend hours on the phone chatting away, and share some of our deepest secrets. For the first time in my life, I felt that the bullying, rejection and troubles were behind me, and I could just be normal like everyone else.

For sixteen years, I had monkeys on my back. I just didn't know it.

"Self awareness involves deep personal honesty. It comes from asking and answering hard questions."
— Stephen Covey

The starting point in taking control and becoming confident, fearless and tough in school and in life is self-awareness. When referring to self-awareness, I'm referring to the things which are holding you back from reaching your full potential, whether it's in the classroom, on the sporting field or on the streets of life.

These things are what I call 'monkeys', because they hang onto you and don't want to leave and make you feel like it's the end of the world. For many teens, these monkeys are sitting comfortably on their backs.

I will introduce these monkeys to you shortly, but let's first explore the importance of self-awareness.

The teenage journey is about personal growth and gaining awareness of the things that are holding you back, so that you can feel empowered to grow and evolve to the next level and achieve great things in your life.

When you become aware of the monkeys in your life and how they are affecting you, you experience not only an internal power and strength from that knowledge, but also a level of awareness and acceptance of why you are currently at where you are at in life.

With greater awareness, it provides you with not only the opportunity to take corrective action and bring an emotional closure to the things that you don't like that are happening in your life, but the opportunity to grow and move forward to unlock your full potential.

"Without self awareness, we are as babies in the cradles."
— Virginia Woolf

If you do not walk through a journey of self-awareness to gain a greater understanding of yourself and the monkeys that are holding you back, you may feel trapped and become imprisoned by your current reality, without your full comprehension and knowledge. It can become damaging to your self-image and mental health, igniting feelings of stress, anxiety and hopelessness. It can also diminish your ability to envision the possibilities and opportunities that are available to you whilst at school and once you leave school, therefore leading to wasted potential.

In more serious cases, constant negative emotions can lead to detrimental and harmful behaviour, like drug taking, alcohol and other negative outlets and relationships as a way to suppress and fulfil these negative emotions. By allowing these monkeys to remain on your back, you'll continue to attract unwanted situations and repeat cycles with people, places and events that will become a downward spiral.

For the remainder of this chapter, I will help you identify the monkeys on your back and how you can increase your level of awareness towards their existence.

For the remaining chapters of this book, I'll be sharing strategies to help you get these monkeys off your back so you can live up to your full potential and succeed academically, socially and emotionally.

Self-awareness of the monkeys on your back comes through what I call 'notifications' or 'alerts', just like those you may receive on social media.

By receiving these notifications, you are saying to yourself, "Yes, I acknowledge where I'm currently at. I know what issues I need to deal with, and the monkeys on my back… and now that I know, I'm going to take action and change." That self-awareness develops your inner power and strength to take corrective action to get the monkeys off your back.

The first type is the **external** notification. As a teen, you are still in the development and dependence stage, so these notifications are many. For example, when a teacher or parent provides advice or feedback to you, this is an externally sourced notification that increases your level of self-awareness about a particular area, like your studies or the people you're hanging out with.

It could come upon request when asking for help or advice, or it may come your way unexpectedly because that person cares about you, which can be harsh sometimes, but it's usually what the doctor ordered. Trust me, I've been there many times. Proactively seeking feedback and advice from people you trust is a great way to increase your self-awareness.

The second type is the **internal** notification, where your self-awareness increases from personal experiences and the lessons learnt upon reflection. Powerful reflection can be achieved through silent meditation and journaling your thoughts and experiences. Some experiences are minor, like that time you said or did something you shouldn't have, and thought to yourself afterwards, "I really shouldn't have said or done that." Some experiences are major, extremely painful and really rock the boat. They became a huge 'wake-up call'.

WAKE-UP CALL

It was just three of us on the footy field – Adrian, Pedro and I – on that late spring afternoon in November. Pedro and I had just finished Year 11. Adrian had left school in Year 10. The sun was setting while we were passing and kicking the football around, running at each other, and just having some fun. I was feeling great. My life was finally coming together and I could bury the struggles of my past.

About an hour into the fun and fitness, Adrian threw the ball at me really hard and threw with it a whole bunch of malicious, spiteful and hurtful words. I was caught on the blind side, completely off guard. For the first five seconds, I was trying to work out whether he was actually serious or not. Maybe he was just joking and paying me out like always, because that's what mates do, right? They pay each other out. I didn't know any better. To my shock, he wasn't joking around.

I couldn't believe my eyes and ears.

Just when I thought the social rejection of the past could be left in the past, in that one moment, it returned and was delivered by the closest people to me at that point in my life. Pedro was just laughing in the background while Adrian was abusing me. He didn't even defend me. I felt like it was planned.

I couldn't take it. Within thirty seconds, I stormed off the field and for the next thirty minutes, I walked home alone, crying like a baby, filled with so much pain and hurt, questioning why it happened and why it happened to me.

During those previous eighteen months, Adrian, Pedro and I were best friends. Well, I thought we were. They didn't. In hindsight, they were always paying me out on a small scale. I just accepted it and let it go for the sake of being liked because I was thirsty for acceptance. I was in denial. They never pushed me forward. They never encouraged me. They never defended me around other people when called upon.

They were fake friends, and that moment of truth came to life on the footy field. I didn't know at the time, but all along, I was in an unhealthy relationship.

The walk home was the longest thirty minutes of my life and where I was at my most vulnerable.

On one hand, I felt like my whole life came crashing down at the death of a fake friendship that I attached my identity to.

On the other, I thought of my parents, and their unconditional love and support over the years. They were the only people who ever really had my back. They were working-class immigrants who sacrificed everything to provide opportunity for their children, something I became grateful for during this time.

As painful as the experience was, it awakened me to the monkeys that had been on my back for years preventing me from reaching my full potential – the bullying, the social exclusion, the people-pleasing, the low self-esteem, the academic disconnection, the lack of motivation, the distractions, ignoring the advice of my loving parents, and the list goes on.

It was a defining moment in my life. I had to make one of two choices – either stay down and allow other people's opinions dictate my reality; or get up, take full control and become the leader of my life.

I had enough. I decided to take control of my life and my future. I decided to not allow other people's opinions dictate my reality. I decided to turn my pain into fuel and prove people wrong. I decided to make my parents proud. I decided to be somebody. I decided to get the monkeys off my back.

Within less than a year, I completely turned my life around.

Academically, I became laser-focused and went from being an average student in Year 11 to being listed in the top 10% of Australia in Year 12.

Socially, I re-evaluated the meaning of true friendship and went from being a people-pleaser to seeking relationships with people who loved me for who I was.

The most important of all – emotionally – where I developed a strong character and resilience in dealing with tough times, shaping me into the person I am today.

I was too young to see it at the time, but looking back now, Oprah's words ring true. Everything really does happen for a reason.

The footy field experience proved to be a blessing in disguise and wake-up call. At sixteen, it became the catalyst that ignited personal change in my final year of school, leading to a life of achievements in adulthood.

THE MONKEYS

"Knowing yourself is the beginning of all wisdom."
— Aristotle

I'd like to now share with you how you can become more self-aware by introducing you to the monkeys.

There are five core monkeys that exist amongst teens today. I have identified these monkeys not only through my journey as a teen, but also from having spoken at many schools and conducting research amongst teachers, parents and students.

The five monkeys are:

1. **Enzo** – the **emotional monkey**
2. **Scooter** – the **social monkey**
3. **Darryl** – the **distracted monkey**
4. **Tyson** – the **tough monkey**
5. **Moi** – the **monkey in the mirror**

Let's get to know each of these monkeys personally. By doing so, we can explore some of the warning signs that will tell you they are on your back.

Enzo
Let's start with **Enzo**, the **emotional monkey**.

Some of the thoughts and feelings that may run through the mind when Enzo is on your back include:

- I'm not smart enough or good enough to be/do/ have…
- OMG, there's no way I could achieve that. I've never done it before
- I'm really scared. I don't want to let my parents/ my teachers/myself down
- OMG, I have no idea what I want to do when I finish school and it's freaking me out
- There's so much pressure to deal with and I'm so stressed
- I can't take this anymore

There are several reasons for these thoughts and feelings to emerge within that you need to be conscious of.

The first reason is the **cancer of comparison**. It's only natural to be drawn into how others look, think, talk, behave, perform and so on, but when interest and admiration towards others turns into jealousy and envy, it becomes emotionally dangerous and easy to fall into the 'why can't I…' trap.

By comparing, it creates negative emotions and stops you from embracing everything about yourself, being grateful for the things you do have as opposed to the things you don't, and making the most of the gifts that you've been given. Comparing leads to feelings of inadequacy and unhappiness, and is a major source of stress and anxiety.

The second reason is **battered belief**, which is usually caused when looking into the rear-view mirror of your life and seeing past failures and disappointments, and becoming discouraged, de-motivated and emotionally disabled to take action to change. You allow yourself to be held back by your past by allowing your past to falsely dictate what's possible for you in the future. Crushing the rear-view mirror is the first step to regaining self-belief.

The third reason is **unmanaged fears, stress and anxiety.** At any age and stage in life, fear will always exist. It's part of being a human being. They pop up in different contexts. The two main types of fears are performance-related fear, such as fear of failure, and social fears, such as the fear of not fitting in.

If you are experiencing performance-related fear, take a moment and ask the following questions:

- What are you scared of and why?
- Are you afraid of failure?
- Are you worried about letting others down?
- Where is the pressure coming from?
- Have your parents placed high expectations on you?
- Are you putting additional pressure on yourself?

If performance-related fears are not managed properly, it leads to stress and anxiety, and has a debilitating effect on your ability to deliver your personal best.

The fourth reason is when **tough times** strike, which are outside of your control. It could be a family illness or death, a personal illness, a family breakdown, a natural disaster or any other situation outside of your direct control. Enzo is clever and will make you feel like it's the end of the world and will encourage you to become a victim of your circumstances, because this will allow him to stay on your back. When teens choose to be a victim, their grades fall, they make irresponsible choices, become associated with the wrong people, and resort to other negative avenues to support their emotional needs.

1. TUNING IN

Scooter
Let's now meet **Scooter**, the **social monkey**.

A major social fear amongst teens is not fitting in, rejection and social disapproval. This is because relationships give meaning to life and provide a sense of belonging. If you were to put aside $1 for every time you worried about what other people think of you, how much money do you think you would rack up? If it's a lot of money, then you might be in a people-pleasing prison.

The fear of disapproval turns into stress and anxiety, and creates pressure – the pressure to conform and please others to feel approved, validated and accepted. Being a people-pleaser is like saying to others, "Hey dude, here is my happiness. I'll leave it up to you what you do with it."

You lose yourself when you constantly feel you need to please others, to fit in, to be cool, to feel validated. It becomes a psychological prison that shapes important choices that can lead to unwanted situations, relationships and pressure – robbing you of personal joy, of being the real you, and of unlocking your potential.

In this cyber age, bullying has become widespread, and affects people in different ways. It's a severe form of allowing others (i.e. bullies) to determine and take control of your happiness. The bully beats you when you give permission to the bully to dictate your thoughts, emotions and reality. There are ways to respond and protect yourself if you are being bullied online and offline, but it's about first choosing to be a *victor*, not a *victim*, of bullying.

Darryl
Let's turn our attention to **Darryl**, the **distracted monkey**.

In a highly advanced, fast-paced and socially connected world, distractions are inevitable and become unhealthy when there is too much of them, or used at the wrong time.

13

Think back to a time when you had an assessment due. You sat down and were ready to go, with your laptop, textbooks and your mobile phone beside you. You check social media notifications every five minutes because your phone keeps lighting up in front of you. Two hours fly by, and you feel like you haven't accomplished much during that time. By having your phone in sight, you've allowed Daryl to reduce your learning experience. Had you kept your phone out of sight and completed your studies, it would not have been a big deal if you received these notifications while unwinding and watching some TV.

Technology has become a weapon of mass distraction in not only school work, but also in family and social relationships. How many times have you been out at a restaurant and see almost every person on the table playing with their phones, checking their feeds, wanting to take photos and videos to share in their 'virtual' world, and missing out on being present in that very moment in the 'real' world? There is nothing wrong with using technology at the right time, but using too much of it and at the wrong time is a recipe for diminished performance, relationships and quality of life, losing touch all together, becoming a recipe for addiction.

Isn't it awesome when you receive a text from a friend saying something like, "Hey, wanna go to the movies?" If you're in Year 12, you've also got 18th birthdays to attend, along with the added freedom of being able to drive. While it may raise your excitement levels, it's another distraction to manage. There is nothing wrong with spending time with friends, going to the movies, birthday parties and so on, but too much time devoted to 'having fun' at the wrong time takes time away from focusing on your school commitments, which is unhealthy and affects your ability to deliver your personal best.

Tyson

Have you ever had the following thoughts and feelings run through your mind?

- No one understands me.
- I don't need any help. I'm perfectly fine.
- No one cares about me.
- I'm afraid of speaking about it.
- I don't know who to talk to.
- If I speak out, what will others think of me?

If you have, then **Tyson**, the **tough monkey,** is hanging on your back. Tyson loves those who travel solo in times when they need to seek help. Help could be in relation to school work, and also extends to more serious issues like dealing with adversity and mental health issues.

Today, there is a rise of mental health issues experienced by teens. There are those who have been diagnosed with a specific illness, and placed on an appropriate support plan, whilst others remain undiagnosed because they have not reached out for help, due to the fear of the stigma attached to speaking out, especially amongst males.

If you are someone who has not asked for help, either because you've been crippled by fear or blinded by pride, then you are getting in the way of your own success and well-being.

No one becomes successful on their own.

Moi

'**Moi**' is a French word, meaning 'Me'.

You'll know from your attitude and motivation levels when **the monkey is staring back at you in the mirror** every morning.

You'll have these thoughts running through your mind:

- I can't be bothered studying, training and practising.
- I'm not academic. I don't give a stuff.
- This is the best time of my life. I'd rather just be having fun.
- Why does this subject matter? Why does school matter anyway?
- This won't apply to me in the future.
- I'm so not interested in school.

"You can lead a horse to water, but you can't get it to drink."
— Proverb

You could be attending the most elite school, with top teachers, and an abundance of opportunities, but they still may not be enough to motivate you to succeed. The opposite can apply, and that's more than enough reasons to be motivated to succeed. Motivation and a winning attitude is an inside job. How thirsty are you?

If you're lacking motivation, remember that a bad attitude is like a flat tire. You can't go anywhere until you change it.

So there they are – the five monkeys.

Do you feel like you have at least one on your back?
Remember, all the monkeys are related, and when one is on your back, the others are more than likely to appear as well. There is one dominant monkey that triggers the others. Monkey breeds monkey. For example, if Enzo is on your

back because you fear social rejection and continuously worry about not fitting in, then it is likely that you are a people-pleaser and influenced by the peer pressure to conform. Therefore, Scooter may also be on your back too.

As you have read this chapter, you may have identified the monkeys on your back, but you may still feel powerless and hopeless with the belief that your problems cannot be solved.

That's okay. I know exactly how you feel, but what I am here to tell you is to be patient and stay tuned, because for the remainder of this book, I'll be equipping you with strategies and sharing real life stories to educate, empower and inspire you to get the monkeys off your back.

This is just the first step: tuning in and defining what's holding you back.

If you feel that you still can't get the monkeys off your back, even after attempting all the exercises recommended in this book and allowing some time for change, then ask for support. Who are the people around you that you trust and can reach out to for help? (see Chapter 3). You can even contact us and we will guide you.

There is a solution to every problem. This book is only a resource to provide you with insight, guidance and perspective. Reading a book doesn't always solve problems immediately, and in most cases, you need to seek face-to-face support. Reading a book is just the start of the process.

If you're worried or feel that you might lose friends as you're changing and growing as a person, do not worry. Life is a journey filled with many changes, so remember the old saying: there are friends for a reason, friends for a season and friends for a lifetime.

Life is not always about fitting in, no matter how old you are. It's about truly being in alignment with your values and aspirations. It's about being at a certain level in your life and truly happy with who you really are. With this, you'll attract those friends who are also energetically aligned and who are at the same level as you are. It's about growing in quality and noticing the people who are drawn to you. The right ones will stick.

It's about just being you.

EXERCISE

Journaling can be super powerful to develop self-awareness, so if you don't already have one, grab yourself a journal and complete the following:

- Identify the monkeys that are holding you back and describe their existence in your life. Which monkey is the most dominant?
- Describe what your life would look like if you got rid of these monkeys.
- List any external and internal notifications that you have received over the past six months. Next to each notification, describe the action you took for each. Be brutally honest with yourself. If ignorance and non-action took place, write it down and the reasons why.

SUMMARY

1. The starting point to becoming confident, fearless and tough in school and in life is self-awareness of the monkeys that are holding you back.

2. There are five monkeys: Enzo, Scooter, Darryl, Tyson and Moi. Being aware of these monkeys will ignite the power and strength within you to take action and get them off your back.

3. Developing greater self-awareness of the monkeys comes from two types of alerts – external notifications, such as a parent, teacher, or friend; or from internal notifications arising from personal experiences and reflection.

2. DIG DEEP, DEEP, DEEP

"What lies behind us and what lies ahead of us are tiny matters compared to what lies within us."
— Ralph Waldo Emerson

*A*t a very young age, Kane arrived in Australia as a refugee. Raised in a low socio-economic household by a single mother who was chronically ill and unable to work, they relied on social welfare to survive. Despite English not being his first language, he was relied upon to be the family interpreter for energy bill disputes and even school enquiries. Kane thought this was normal until high school, when he realised his peers did not have the same challenges and most were better off financially.

A great talker and street smart, Kane was an average student, just wanting to have fun and never taking his studies seriously. While his peers were consistently studying, Kane lacked discipline and a work ethic. He thought studying was boring and didn't understand why his peers would put themselves through boring things. For Kane, the less structure, the better. He was impulsive and wouldn't prepare for exams, relying on natural intelligence to get him through, something he took pride in. Kane didn't recognise the importance of education and couldn't wait to get out of school.

At fourteen, Kane's identity was rattled when he discovered that his brother, Simon, was only a half-brother, and that they didn't share the same father. Kane became extremely angry and bitter towards his family, especially his mother, for not telling him earlier. The news shook the foundations of who he thought he was. Feeling embarrassed, he disconnected from Simon and his family.

Not knowing who his real father was, Kane felt lost, and his sense of self had evaporated. Filled with anger, he became academically disconnected even further after the incident. He isolated himself and began digging deep, asking himself, 'Is Mum really Mum?' and 'Who am I really?'

At some point, just like Kane, the 'who am I' question will be staring right back at you.

Your teen years are your foundational development years – physically, emotionally and socially. It's a time of self-discovery, as you transition from adolescence to adulthood, from dependence to independence.

It's a journey about discovering the fullness of truth – the truth of your **identity**, **worth** and **potential**. This chapter will focus on identity only. The following two chapters will delve into the truth of your worth and potential.

Discovering your true identity is similar to when a gold miner is searching for gold. They search by digging deep into the ground. The deeper they dig, the greater the chances of finding gold. If the gold miner looks around and starts digging wide, the chances of finding gold are frail.

By digging deep, you'll gain a deeper understanding of your personality traits, what you're good at, not good at, your values and what you value, what you're passionate about, what motivates you, what gives you joy, and also the monkeys that are holding you back.

This knowledge shapes the choices you make in *school* (e.g. subject selections, extracurricular activities, career pathways), *socially* (friendships, social circles, dating), and out of *personal preference* (e.g. hobbies, fashion taste, religious beliefs). It becomes a source of strength and guidance to make the right choices that are aligned to your interests, strengths, beliefs and values. Your true identity will lead you to finding your purpose.

Knowing yourself creates a defensive shield around you when peer pressure, bullying or negative people strike, which can steer you away from situations that need to be avoided because they do not align to your beliefs and values. You won't have that awkward feeling like the shoes you are wearing don't fit because what you feel, say, believe, value and do is synced. You'll be able to say loud and confidently, "I know myself. I know who I am." This is one of the greatest feelings and achievements of life.

You often hear people being told to discover who they are, but it's not as easy as turning on the TV. It's also a difficult question to answer without acknowledging who you are not.

Over a lifetime, a person will usually experience at least two of the following:

1. Identity Truth – "I **know** who I am and I know who I am not."
2. Identity Illusion – "I **think** I know who I am."
3. Identity Crisis – "I **do not know** who I am."

If you do not discover your identity truth, either an identity illusion or identity crisis will take effect.

In search of acceptance and presence, most teens create an identity by attaching themselves to something or someone outside of themselves like a group of friends, popularity, sport, grades, body image, music preference, culture, trends, possessions, dating. Teens also attach themselves to and become reliant on confidence-building labels for identity, like cool, popular, smart, talented, good-looking and rich.

These attachments become part of who you believe you are; however, these can also lead to identity illusion because these attachments are temporary and can change at any point. When your identity is defined by what is temporary, it becomes dangerous when you lose it. You feel ripped apart and lost. You lose your sense of self, and give birth to an identity crisis.

An **unattached identity** is created on truth and authenticity, built from within you, not around you, and one that evolves with education and experience. Your identity is not defined by people, things, appearances, results, and events. You are more than temporary confidence-building attachments.

"The greatest challenge in life is discovering who you are. The second greatest is being happy with what you find."
— Unknown

For over a year, Kane would play the same scenarios relating to his family situation over and over in his mind, fuelling his anger, sadness and bitterness. It dominated his thinking, clouded his judgment, and stopped him from taking opportunities at school. It affected the quality of his friendships because he was not being himself. Kane was not living – he was barely surviving.

As a young male, Kane was not accustomed to speaking about his problems and disconnected himself from others, leading to loneliness and sadness, especially when Simon moved away. Feeling broken kept his focus on his problems, rather than igniting the person he truly was on the inside. Kane was heading towards depression if he kept holding onto the anger about his family situation any longer.

At fifteen, Kane decided to step out of his comfort zone to experience new things. Rather than hold onto anger, he channelled his energy towards a positive outlet by joining the local Police Citizens Youth Club (PCYC) and learning breakdancing, which allowed him to meet new people and develop positive relationships, and provided him with fresh experiences and perspectives about life. Kane felt reinvigorated and rediscovered talents, skills and abilities that he already had, such as the ability to connect with people, as well as new discoveries like his enjoyment of public speaking.

The PCYC environment allowed Kane to meet police officers and developed a good relationship with one in particular named Jason. Simply by having a positive relationship with Jason, Kane was motivated to remain on a positive track to avoid disappointing Jason.

For the next ten years, Kane's breakdancing crew became his family, creating an empowering environment that was forward-looking and not based on personal history and shame. The journey was cleansing, as it allowed Kane to move forward and focus on the things he could influence, rather than being held back by the things he couldn't control or change.

Along the journey, Kane learned more about his personality and values, especially when he chose to be compassionate towards his mother even while still filled with anger. An eternal optimist by nature, he chose a path of contribution rather than retribution, undertaking various school and community leadership roles and volunteered his time to contribute to positive community projects, such as teaching dance classes and hosting events for local young people. In Year 11, Kane's English teacher nominated him for a place in the student council. Later he was selected as school captain.

Shaped by his upbringing, Kane's foundational beliefs and values were to help and to give to others. Growing up, his mother didn't heavily push education as the single goal, but encouraged him to always give. This established his empathy and compassion for others. During his late teens, Kane was motivated by a deep sense of belonging and felt proud when seeing the joy on youthful faces involved in the projects he led and contributed towards.

Over time, Kane accepted his family history and embraced them as part of his identity and life story. Rather than viewing it as a weakness, he saw his experience as a strength and the opportunity to build his character.

From digging deep, Kane discovered his S.T.U.F.F. and the truth of his identity.

DISCOVERING YOUR S.T.U.F.F.

For the remainder of this chapter, I will walk you through how you can dig deep to discover your true unattached identity. Finding identity truth is about uncovering the five elements that make and shape you to be the person you are.

These five elements are your *Strengths, Temperament, Uniqueness, Foundation* and *Flaws.* This is your S.T.U.F.F. and it comprises your genetic makeup, the gifts you were born with, and the things you have acquired through education, experience and natural growth.

Strengths

Your strengths are the *talents, skills and abilities* you've *already discovered* in your life to date. They also include your personal qualities – such as integrity, loyalty, compassion, determination and ambition – that make up your character.

Discovering these strengths requires taking time out. Teens get caught up in the noise of their environment that they never make time for reflection.

Write down a list of strengths that you've already discovered about yourself. Include your passions and interests – the things that draw you in, ignite curiosity and bring you to life. They give you energy and enjoyment and you lose track of time when doing them. You excel when you put your strengths to work. For example, it could be music, art, computers, writing, problem solving, using your hands to make something, helping the poor.

Tune in to the compliments that others have given you about these things. Reflect on your past achievements to date, whether big and small. These are all clues and seeing this list in front of you is motivating. It will increase your confidence, self-love and self-acceptance for who you are.

If you are getting stuck, approach someone you trust and respect, not just anyone, and ask for their thoughts and opinion. Confirmation by trusted individuals is always refreshing that you're on the right track with the strengths you believe in.

Your strengths include that which you have *yet to discover* – the talents and abilities you never knew you had. This requires you to step out and explore, experiment and experience different things. It may require courage, especially if it is outside of your comfort zone, but it's the only way to unlock your potential. You discover from doing, not sitting on the sidelines. Keep in mind that whenever discovering something for the first time will not mean that you are the world's best at it. You will only get really good by working on it. That's why there are endless opportunities when you identify areas that interest you, and while you may not be the very best initially, you can always develop these skills with work.

Temperament
Your temperament refers to your personality type.

Do you prefer talking or listening, routine or variety, being with a large or small group of people, leading or following, creativity or numerical problem solving, working individually or in a team?

Some personalities complement each other, whilst others are complete opposites. Sometimes it's one of the reasons why some people get along like a house on fire, while others always clash.

Knowing your temperament provides a deeper understanding of why you think, act, behave, speak and deal with others the way you do, especially in moments when you may think that you're 'weird' or 'different'.

By knowing your temperament, you will no longer feel the internal pressure to be like someone else in social settings. For example, you'll no longer question why you're the introverted or quiet person at a teen party while those around you are much louder, dominant and out there. It's just who you are and who they are. Life wouldn't be so interesting if everyone had the same personality, so embrace yours.

By acknowledging your temperament, you'll find it easier to understand and deal with others because you have the ability to acknowledge their temperament too.

Uniqueness

Many factors shape a person's uniqueness – experiences, genetics, beliefs, morals, attitude, physicality, tastes, ambition, culture and so forth. For this reason, you are like no other – an original, special and one of a kind. No one can speak, blink, breathe, walk, write, type, sing, think, and love the way you do.

What is your trademark that others always remember you by?
It could be your sense of humour, your laughter, your bubbliness, your social and entertaining nature, your care and warmth and so forth.

Being yourself and allowing your uniqueness to shine will only make you happier and confident, but when you try and copy someone else, it's like trying to wear a different sized pair of shoes to what matches your feet. If you wear it, you'll experience pain, pressure and stress. Wearing someone else's shoe never fits. You can't compare or copy uniqueness. It's a lost battle before you begin.

Stay true to who you are, despite the background noise of what people, trends or culture suggests.

Foundation

"If you don't stand for something, you'll fall for anything."
— Malcolm X

Your beliefs are the things you stand for. When your beliefs are strong enough, they become your values, the things important to you in life, like family, friends, faith, and form the foundation of your identity. Without strong beliefs, you can be easily led astray, taken advantage of, and seek identity through the beliefs of others.

Beliefs and values can change over time and are shaped by your:

- **education** received at home, school or society
- **environment** (friends, social media, culture and social trends)
- **experiences** encountered growing up and personal interest discoveries
- **examples** (both positive and negative) set by others

As you grow through your teen years, you are constantly learning new things about yourself, others and life. During this time, you're more socially conscious of your identity, and your priorities may change, and the values that were instilled in you at home at a young age are either supported, challenged, or replaced by new things that become important to you, like fitting in, popularity, social media, body image, materialism, culture and trends. Your values determine your priorities in life, and these dictate your decisions.

A common scenario for teens is when the values instilled by parents during childhood are challenged by instances of peer pressure, what the 'cool' thing to do is. Some are resilient and stand by their values, while others choose to wear a mask and steer away from what they've always known because social acceptance becomes the thing they value the most.

You live an authentic identity when the decisions you make are aligned to your foundational beliefs and values. Everyone has different beliefs and values, but what's important is to know your rock solid values, the things you will never compromise for anyone and anything. This shapes your character.

If you feel you have a weak foundation of beliefs and values, review the factors mentioned above that have shaped them, such as the people you hang with, and replace negative influences with positive influences. You will see a change in your outlook towards life.

Flaws

"Don't forget to fall in love with yourself first."
— Carrie Bradshaw

Teens tend to focus more on becoming someone else's best friend first than becoming their own. Becoming your own best friend is about accepting that you are not perfect. You never were, never will be, and were never meant to be. It's easy to identify the things you're not good at or the times you messed up.

Don't be ashamed of your flaws. Acknowledging them and showing self-compassion only strengthens your acceptance for who you are, in spite of your imperfections. This builds a strong identity and inner security that stops you from beating yourself up or allowing others to because of your mistakes or weaknesses. You went through those experiences for a reason. One day, you'll be able to turn your flaws into strengths, and use your story to inspire and help others. Remember, a story is worthless if remained untold.

DISCOVERING YOUR PURPOSE

"... as with all matters of the heart, you'll know when you find it."
— Steve Jobs

At twenty-three, I became a Chartered Accountant (CA). I had a great job with one of Australia's leading accounting firms, where I managed multi-million dollar client portfolios.

I was living it – living the dream that I had since school to become a corporate professional. I could wear an expensive-looking suit and work in a high rise building in the heart of Sydney overlooking the amazing views.

Despite the success, I wasn't passionate about the path I was on, and often felt unfulfilled, empty and looking for answers.

At twenty-four, I stepped out and explored new things. I became more involved with my church's youth group and was selected to be the NSW event coordinator. In this role, I discovered talents, skills and abilities that I never knew I had, including leadership, connecting with people, sales and a passion for public speaking, given my extroverted personality. These formed part of my strengths, temperament and uniqueness.

In the same year, I hosted a youth event of four-hundred people. It was the first time ever picking up the microphone. Needless to say, it wasn't the best display of public speaking, but that experience lit an internal spark and set my heart on fire. It allowed me to start dreaming again and the possibilities of becoming a professional speaker.

Several years passed where nothing happened. I continued on my corporate path yet the flame within still kept on burning.

At twenty-eight, after a life-changing experience hiking the famous Machu Picchu, I decided to pursue my passion. Immediately after returning to Australia, I embarked upon the professional speaking journey, initially as a Master of Ceremonies (MC).

While on this journey, I kept hearing an inner whisper calling me to become a teen inspirational speaker. Despite having never spoken to a teen audience before, my heart was drawing me towards this path, and I felt called to share some of the darkest days of my life to bring light to others, even though the experiences formed part of my flaws.

As this inner whisper became louder and louder over time, I received more signs, including encouragement from my circle of support.

One day, I received a random message on my Facebook page. It was from the Year 12 deputy coordinator at my former school, inviting me back to speak to students, who were just a few months out from sitting their final exams. I checked the date. It happened to be my birthday. I thought to myself, 'What an awesome birthday gift – the gift of opportunity to inspire students at my former school.'

Just moments before walking on stage to speak on my birthday, an inner voice whispered, 'You were born to speak,' and this empowered me to deliver my first presentation to a teen audience. From the feedback, it was a huge success, with many students approaching me afterwards to chat.

The Year 12 head coordinator commended me, and strongly encouraged me to continue on the path, sharing words of advice from his extensive experience in Pastoral Care. He breathed belief in me, which provided further evidence in support of my inner whisper to take a leap of faith into unknown territory.

"The two most important days in your life are the day you are born and the day you find out why."
— Mark Twain

My S.T.U.F.F allowed me to discover my passion and led me to discovering my true calling – the reason I was born. It didn't happen in one moment. It came through a sequence of events and through a combination of internal and external messages of reinforcement.

Looking back, I realised there was a purpose to every stage of my life, and discovered that purpose can change over time.

When in Year 12, knuckling down to achieve allowed me to fulfil my purpose as a son, by making my parents proud, and setting up a foundation that allowed me to support them financially in later years.

When in my twenties working in senior management, I was fulfilling my purpose as a leader, empowering my team and making a positive contribution to my company.

And now, in writing this book, I'm fulfilling the purpose I've been called to at this stage of my life in inspiring the current and next generation of teens.

I'm regularly asked by teens, how do I find my purpose?

Finding your true calling takes time, and requires constant tuning in with your thoughts, feelings and desires. It's usually not written in the sky or on a billboard. When you do find it, you'll light up inside, feel invigorated, motivated and excited. Others will compliment, support and guide you. You'll feel the impact you're having on other people.

Even if you haven't yet found your true calling, there are opportunities every day to find meaning and purpose in your life. It doesn't have to be big and about changing the world. Examples include providing comfort to a friend going through personal issues, helping your family around the house, standing up for victims of bullying, setting the right example, helping people in need, and brightening up someone's day.

If you feel lost and confused and believe that your life has no purpose, that's not true. Just like the sun was made for light, you were born with a purpose. It's okay not to know. Your purpose is to find your purpose. Every person's journey is different and unique.

Be clear about your passions and determine how you can use them to make a positive difference. When your actions lead to fulfilment, you have found purpose.

"If you can't figure out your purpose, figure out your passion. For your passion will lead you right into your purpose."
— T.D Jakes

STILL NOT SURE?

If you're still not sure of your true identity, even after attempting the recommended exercise, don't panic. It's quite common and normal, as you are still in your development years. I would recommend doing the exercise alongside a trusted adult.

Many adults go through their entire life not accepting the responsibility of discovering who they really are and live life always seeking external validation, never truly being happy and fulfilled. By deciding to discover, you've put yourself on the front foot. Be patient, be curious and always be open to new things, because life is a continuous journey of self-discovery.

EXERCISE

Complete the following:

- Assess your current identity. In doing so, consider whether you are living with identity truth, identity illusion or identity crisis, listing any attachments (e.g. grades, sport, group of friends, popularity, body image) and describing how they have shaped your current identity.
- Conduct a S.T.U.F.F analysis of yourself. Remember to give detail for each component.

- After you complete your S.T.U.F.F analysis, write a list of things you can do, no matter how small, to i) put your current strengths to work and ii) step outside of your comfort zone to develop new skills and discover talents and abilities you never knew you had.

SUMMARY

1. One of life's greatest discoveries is knowing who you really are and living with identity truth. Without it, you'll either live with identity illusion or an identity crisis.

2. Identity truth is found by digging deep and discovering your S.T.U.F.F – your strengths, temperament, uniqueness, foundation and flaws. It doesn't happen overnight. It takes time, reflection and a willingness to step out to experience, learn, and grow.

3. Your S.T.U.F.F is your purpose compass, directing you to the path that will set your heart on fire to create a meaningful and fulfilling life.

3. FREEDOM TO CHOOSE

"Where we end up in life is the sum of the choices that we make along the way."
— Anonymous

With her mother being Pakistani Muslim and father being Hindu, Shammah felt out of place growing up, pressured to conform to cultural expectations, and without a sense of belonging to either culture. At one point, her mother grabbed all her clothes that were deemed culturally 'inappropriate' and burned them. Shammah fell into an identity crisis at a very young age.

At twelve, she was diagnosed with bulimia and severe depression, after putting on 25kg while struggling to cope with her family breakdown. During her teens, Shammah not only experienced a poor body image and eating disorder, but also a self-esteem crisis, learning difficulties at school, unhealthy relationships, and became a target for bullying given her weight and ethnicity. Constantly comparing herself to others, Shammah rejected herself and became her own worst enemy.

Shammah was carrying a damaged self image, an unhealthy relationship with herself, and felt stuck.

Just like Shammah, many teens feel stuck, carrying a damaged self-image from issues such as body image disorders, family breakdowns, failed relationships, failures, constant comparing, bullying and depression. Their deep-rooted value as human beings has been clouded.

Did you know that the reason why one student has a high self-worth is the same reason why another student has a low self-worth? That reason is relationships – with parents, teachers, peers, partners, coaches, relatives and most importantly, the relationship with yourself.

Just like your body needs food to survive, the desire to be loved, appreciated, accepted and respected need to be fulfilled by relationships for life to have meaning and purpose. Relationships are food for your emotions, and

41

can be healthy or unhealthy. Healthy relationships create positive outcomes and high self-worth, whilst unhealthy relationships create negative outcomes and low self-worth.

When you discover the truth of your worth, you'll be empowered to break free of the people-pleasing prison. You'll 'stop caring' about what others think, and 'start caring' about yourself. You'll develop courage to stand up for what you believe in when everyone around you is telling you otherwise. You'll become 'really cool', because when you are able to stand strong under pressure and say no in the heat of the moment, that's being 'cool'.

You'll be happier when you are not afraid to show the world who you are, and won't feel the need to wear a mask. You'll find greater meaning, fulfilment and purpose on your journey. You'll feel safer in your own skin, become harder to hurt, and attract opportunities and the right people into your life who love you for who you are. You'll be strengthened to avoid the most lethal cancer rippling through the digital world today – the **cancer of comparison**.

Without truth, it's easy when in a weak emotional state to fall into the trap of people-pleasing to fill the emotional void, feeding your hungry emotions through unhealthy outlets, and always having to prove yourself to be liked and accepted. This only opens doors to unwanted situations, people and places.

For the remaining parts of this chapter, two relationships will be delved deeper into: the relationship with your peers, and the one with yourself. This chapter will reflect upon the impact they have on your self-image, re-evaluate the meaning of these relationships, and the action you need to take to create healthy relationships and to discover the truth of your worth.

THE GREATEST LOVE

Once, a grandfather wanted to teach his grandson some life lessons, so he said to him, "Grandson, there's a major battle taking place within me. There's a battle between two wolves. The first wolf is a bad wolf filled with anger, bitterness, resentment, fear, anxiety, and stress. The second wolf is a good wolf filled with love, compassion, belief and confidence."

The grandson replied, "Okay, Granddad," and walked away for a few minutes to think about what his grandfather said. He then returned and asked, "So Granddad, which wolf will win?" "The one you feed," the grandfather responded.

Till her early teens, Shammah constantly fed the bad wolf, always feeling not good enough and worthless. Flicking through girl magazines and comparing her body to models also didn't help.

At fifteen, Shammah became more self-aware to the harmful effects of negative self-talk and her eating disorder, and decided to change her life.

First, Shammah started to exercise, and lost 20kgs. Through exercise, she became empowered, healed old wounds, reshaped her self-image and most importantly, started to love herself again.

Second, Shammah stopped comparing herself to others. At one point, she threw all her teen magazines in the bin, stood in front of the mirror and promised herself to mute the negative voices of other people and to redirect her attention to her needs and the action she could take to improve her life.

She became more appreciative of the things she did have rather than what she didn't, and used that to improve her life.

Third, she stopped caring about others who didn't have her best interests, and chose herself first. She took control of her inner voice, feeding it with positivity and truth, one step at a time, no matter how small. Deliberately feeding the good wolf cultivated a healthy relationship with herself, feelings of acceptance rather than rejection, igniting greater confidence.

The relationship with yourself is the most important of all. You're in control as to what type of relationship it is. Self-love is developed by feeding the good wolf through daily, purposeful thoughts and actions. It's just like having a shower. While self-love is developed over time, it's still a choice.

What's the one thing that always seems to bring you down?
Are you looking back at past failures? Current grades? Hating your body image? Being put down by your peers, family members and teachers?

What positive action can you take to change your current state to feed the good wolf?
For body image, it could be to start exercising like Shammah did. If you have poor grades, you'll need to review why and seek assistance from teachers to help you improve where you are struggling.

Just by taking action, you are making a statement to yourself by saying, "I am important to me, and I will do all I can to produce the best version of myself." Without action, nothing will change, and the bad wolf will be fed by default.

Revisit the self-discovery exercise from the previous chapter. In writing down your strengths, how did it make you feel? Proud? Confident? Inspired? Grateful? Own these feelings.

Reflect on past achievements where you've put those strengths to work, even things like avoiding a risky situation, solving a problem and helping other people. How does it make you feel? Own those feelings.

Visualise how you can use your strengths in the future. Not in one, two, five years, but immediately to create confidence boosters.

CUT OUT THE CANCER

"Comparison is an act of violence against the self."
— Iyanla Vanzant

With internet access today at your fingertips, it makes it easy to constantly compare things like body image, popularity, academic results or sporting achievements, and all the materialistic stuff. To be interested in and admire others is one thing, but to constantly compare yourself to others gives birth to the cancer of comparison.

Social media feeds only show life 'highlights', not the 'whole package' (the highs and lows). If you compare your life (the 'whole package') to the lives of others (the 'highlights') as a measure of your own value, you will lose every time, because you will naturally be drawn to the things you don't have that others do, rather than the things you do have that others don't. It blinds you from seeing your uniqueness, and only feeds the bad wolf with confidence-crushing messages, leading to feelings of inadequacy.

Anita was born premature, walked differently, and was judged as someone needing constant physical and intellectual care. A social outcast, everywhere she walked others would point and laugh at her. Teachers would put her down indirectly by implying that she couldn't run, when others could, and was not allowed to take part in sports carnivals.

Growing up, she struggled to love herself and constantly compared her life to others. Her confidence was low, lacked motivation, and often felt depressed. At times, she didn't want to live. Some days would go by where she would not speak at all.

When Anita, at sixteen, stopped comparing lives, it ended her inner struggle and freed her to redirect her attention to the blessings in her life, like a supportive family, faith in God and her untapped potential. While she couldn't walk like others, there were things that she could do that others couldn't. Focusing on her S.T.U.F.F increased self worth.

With a newfound level of confidence in herself, Anita wanted to show others that she was more than just her physical condition and that she was capable of achieving whatever she put her mind to, so she started putting effort into her studies and saw positive changes within herself and her results.

Along the way, Anita maintained positive relationships that encouraged her and fuelled her self-belief. She started studying with one friend, Mary, who had a strong and confident personality. Mary encouraged her, gave her study hints and tips, and made her feel more confident.

Whenever Anita appeared to be lacking motivation, Mary would give encouraging words like, "You can do better than that, Anita". Her parents never gave her special treatment and constantly reminded her that she could do everything that they can do.

Anita did face challenges during her transformational journey, one in particular from a negative friend, Vanessa. Despite seeing the positive change in Anita, Vanessa would deliberately bring up the past to bring Anita down. The resilient mindset that Anita developed allowed her to redirect her focus to the positive influences around her, while at the same time she showed compassion towards Vanessa by encouraging and supporting her to turn her life around as well.

Anita became her own best friend.

Think twice the next time you fall into the trap of comparing and begin beating yourself up.

If you do fall into the trap of comparison, stop and ask yourself these questions:

Am I willing to take the 'whole package', and not just the 'highlights'?
The grass is not always greener on the other side.

Why do I get to have these gifts/these people/these experiences in my life?
Having that attitude of gratitude will train your mind to focus on the things you do have, and not on the things you don't. This will help you avoid the 'why can't I…' trap.

Am I using 'external variables' to measure my self worth?
External variables – like body image, grades, popularity, material possessions – are temporary and can change over time, as seen in Shammah's story. Show self-compassion and redirect your attention to the personal qualities you have, such as loyalty, integrity, and generosity.

Seek internal not external validation. By doing so, you are setting the standard about your own self-worth and self-approval, and not basing your value on what you see and hear around you. By setting the standard from within, the outside world can either support it or reject it. You will attract the right people in your life, because how you value yourself is a reflection of how you value others.

THE TRUTH WILL SET YOU FREE

When I was in Year 11, Melio, an old student, visited my school. I hadn't seen Melio since Year 8. We had a good chat in the playground, exchanged numbers and kept in contact from time to time.

After the footy field experience shared in chapter one, I re-evaluated the meaning of friendship. I realised that the friendship I thought I had with Adrian and Pedro was actually fake and unhealthy, because I was always seeking their acceptance and wanting them to like me. I was never good enough, yet I held on because I feared rejection. When I was made fun of or ridiculed, I would let it go, hoping they wouldn't do it again. Time revealed the hard truth on the footy field, but it set me free from the people-pleasing prison.

Melio and I remained in contact and became closer. As difficult as Year 12 was, he supported me and breathed hope and joy into my life. My self-worth was restored because of him. I felt free because he was a true friend and I could just be myself around him.

Have you ever thought about what defines a true friend? Consider the following:

- Do they love you unconditionally or are they hanging out with you because they are using you for something?
- Do they continually encourage and support you in a positive way?
- Would they put your life at risk?

- Can you freely be yourself when around them?
- Will they have your back when the going gets tough?

For most, friends become more important than family during teen years, and their opinions matter more to you that the opinion of parents and teachers. You become very protective of your circle. The desire to be liked becomes a matter of social survival.

The truth is that the majority of the people you're currently hanging around will not be around you when you leave school. Ask any adult as to how many old school friends they still maintain regular phone and face-to-face communication with, not including social media, and most will respond with one or two. That's life. One true friend is better than a circle of fake friends.

"A 'No' uttered from the deepest conviction is better than a 'Yes' uttered merely to please, or worse, avoid trouble."
— Mahatma Gandhi

When becoming more socially active in your teen years, you'll have new experiences, like attending birthday parties, movie nights, camping and dating. Scenarios will arise where there are certain expectations and pressures to look, dress, speak and behave in a certain way to fit in. These expectations and pressures range from smoking, drinking alcohol, having sex, experimenting with drugs, to engaging in social bullying and exclusion, sexting, cyber-bullying, skipping school, being involved in violence and gangs or any form of illegal activity.

It's okay to say no to fake relationships, to risking your life, and to the pressure to be someone that you're not. Life is not about fitting in. It's about setting the standard based on your values, and the right people will befriend, support and follow you.

Some of these choices are life and death. It's not worth risking your life for the sake of being 'cool'. Before every choice you make, pause and ask yourself, 'Am I putting my life at risk? Is there danger involved?'

Once the choice is made, there is no turning back. It's set in stone. You can't just Ctrl Alt Delete and pretend it didn't happen. Think about your loved ones and the people who will be affected by your choice. Asking yourself those questions provide a different perspective that can be a lifesaver.

DITCH THE DEAD END

"If you sleep with dogs, you wake up with fleas."
— Proverb

Born to migrant parents, Raj was raised in a toxic and unstable home environment. His father was a chronic alcoholic, and growing up, Raj often felt neglected, and had low self-worth.

During his early teens, Raj developed a group of friends in search of love and acceptance that wasn't received at home. He wanted acceptance and got it from peer pressure, because at the time, he couldn't find it anywhere else. He wanted to fit in, so he took the opportunity and felt he didn't have an alternative. He didn't know any better because it was serving him emotionally and making him feel worthy. Despite the group filling this void, they led him down a path of skipping school, gang violence, drugs and alcohol. After being suspended in Year 10 for skipping school, Raj was heading down a dead-end path.

It took one conversation with a caring teacher to spark a change in Raj's attitude. Sharing experiences from a similar upbringing, his teacher shared how educating himself was his ticket out of a cycle of negative environments and influences, and stressed the importance of family rather than friends. He challenged Raj to think about the path he was on, his goals and ambitions, and reminded him of the opportunities available to him to steer away from a dead-end path of people-pleasing, violence, gangs and drugs, and towards a prosperous path focussed on education to enable him to realise his full potential. Raj's teacher lit the spark in his heart and mind that empowered him to change his path, starting with his relationships.

New possibilities were created and Raj started believing. He stopped being a people-pleaser and distanced himself from those dragging him down. It was difficult at first, feeling neglected from time to time in their absence and not receiving the sense of belonging and brotherhood they provided for most of his teens.

While Raj was turning his life around at sixteen, his friends remained on a dead-end path. They were either expelled, in juvenile detention or dead, with the most impactful event being the drive-by shooting death of his closest friend.

It made him realise that the peer relationships he had during his teens, despite filling the emotional void with feelings of acceptance, were unhealthy, eventually leading to destructive consequences. Raj's destiny was different to his peers, not by chance, but by choice.

Many teens fear rejection, and, to avoid it, remain in unhealthy relationships. Teens get themselves into these relationships to fill the emotional void that's missing in their life. These toxic relationships not only apply with peers, but also in intimate relationships. Just because you are being fed with love and acceptance from someone does not always mean it is healthy. Like Raj, it could be unhealthy food with dire consequences.

Think ahead before wanting to fit in, be liked, accepted and validated.

Consider the following:

- Where will this path take you?
- Are your relationships encouraging you to move forward, grow and succeed, or are they holding you back to meet their expectations?
- Fast forward five to ten years down the track. Do you still want to be in the same position? Will you be happy with continuing to live as a people-pleaser?
- Are you putting your friends first before yourself?
- Are you confident that your friends will be around you in the future?
- How can you redirect your time, energy, and search for love and fulfilment to a positive source, starting with yourself?
- Where do you want to be in the future?

If your relationships are not helping you get to where you want to be, then it's time to change.

WINGS TO FLY

"We cannot change the cards we are dealt, just how
we play the hand."
— Randy Pausch

Other than your immediate family, your relationships exist by choice, not by chance. They determine your level of self-worth and destiny.

You have the freedom to choose relationships that elevate and empower you to discover your true self-worth, or relationships that weaken you and lead you down a dead-end path.

Shammah experienced several unhealthy relationships till her mid teens. From being attached to a group of girls who all came from broken families, had poor self-image to instances of peer pressure to conform into something she wasn't, these relationships were filled with cattiness, bullying and trauma.

Not wanting to lose herself, Shammah's destiny changed when she changed who she hung out with. She distanced herself from girls who were bitchy. She found peace, guidance and love from adults, especially from her godmother, who mentored and helped her reframe her perspective and the choices between right and wrong.

Adults saw qualities in her that she couldn't see, giving her belief and enabling her to appreciate her uniqueness, and to celebrate who she was, rather than hating what she was not.

"A healthy relationship will never require you to sacrifice your friends, your dreams and your dignity."
— Mandy Hale

It's not too late to start a fresh page.

Do not fear loneliness if you walk away from unhealthy relationships. Loneliness is not a circumstance, but a choice. There are endless opportunities to step out, meet new people and make new friends who will love and accept the real you, just the way you are.

Reach out to those whom you share a common interest with. It could be music, sport, arts, church and so forth. This extends to beyond the school yard. Think about getting involved in organisations and places that align with your passions (e.g. youth and sporting clubs).

If you feel a sense of hopelessness when you look at your existing circle, do not be afraid to reach out to youth support organisations that exist for the sole purpose of helping teens who are experiencing difficult times.

I would strongly suggest reaching out to one of the youth support organisations listed at the end of this book. You have the freedom to choose, and only you can exercise that freedom.

"Freedom of choice is more to be treasured than any possession earth can give."
— David O'Mckay

It all comes down to choices. The choice of positive self-talk over negative self-talk, the choice to love yourself rather than people-please, the choice to maintain true friends not fake friends, and the choice to have supportive relationships not toxic relationships. Positive relationships will uncover the truth of your worth.

EXERCISE

Complete the following:

- Create a list of confidence boosters that you can take action in daily in order to feed the good wolf and develop greater self-love and self confidence.

  Examples of daily habits include:
  - listening to a regular playlist of positive music and messages (YouTube has plenty)
  - going for a run every morning
  - writing down either three things you love about yourself, did well that day or a personal quote before going to sleep each night.
  - reflecting on past achievements, and visualising dreams and aspirations
- Complete the questions shared earlier relating to what defines a true friend with application to your current friends. In doing so, consider the questions raised under 'Ditch the Dead End'. This requires being brutally honest, and not living in denial. Are you a people-pleaser?

  Once complete, if you've highlighted unhealthy relationships and fake friends, write down a list of things you can do immediately to cut out unhealthy relationships and, in turn, develop positive relationships.

- Use the Circle of Support diagram illustrated earlier and replace categories of people (i.e. family, friend, teacher) with specific names. Once complete, identify three people from this circle and visualise how you would approach them with your current issues, questions and seeking help. Describe how you would like them to support you.

SUMMARY

1. Relationships are food for your emotions, and can be healthy or unhealthy. You have the freedom to choose the food you eat.

2. The most important relationship that you develop, nurture and grow is the one with yourself. The more you love yourself, the better you develop the relationships you have with others, and the better your ability will be to successfully handle peer pressure situations and to avoid a dead-end path.

3. Seek internal not external validation to avoid constantly comparing yourself to others. Comparison will only feed the bad wolf with confidence-crushing messages, leading to feelings of inadequacy.

4. UNLIMITED

"Life is God's gift to you. What you do with that life is
your gift to God."
— Anonymous

Growing up, Nathan was just a kid who loved playing footy. At fifteen, he was described as Australia's next Rugby League superstar, having already secured a signed contract with a leading National Rugby League (NRL) club. Super talented with a personal running best of 10.83 seconds over 100 metres, Nathan was destined for great things.

With humble beginnings, Nathan's world was rocked early on. Just after birth, his father left the family. At the age of three, he tragically lost his mother on his birthday, leaving his grandmother and aunt to raise him and his brother. Without parents, growing up was extremely difficult and traumatic.

After being signed at fifteen, Nathan left home and went to boarding school. While it was tough for him to leave his family, it was a great change of environment, away from the negative crowds in his hometown.

Seemingly on top of the world at sixteen, adversity struck when Nathan severely injured his shoulder and was unable to play for the remainder of the season. He moved back home to be with family and recover. For the next eighteen months, Nathan became severely depressed, feeling useless and worthless due to injury. His sense of identity was shattered.

Not knowing how to deal with his issues at such a young age, Nathan began looking for outlets to fill the emotional void so he started hanging around the wrong crowd in his home town, only to lead him down an addictive and destructive path of alcohol and drugs. Having not played football for almost two years, it was a very difficult time for Nathan, and he began losing hope in the possibility of ever being able to play professional rugby league again.

On many occasions during this low period, Nathan would often hear comments made by older relatives, such as, "He could have been something special", "He's too good to be playing back home", "Such wasted talent" and "He threw everything away."

Nathan was super talented, but that was not enough. He was missing the keys to unlock the truth of his potential.

When thinking of potential, visualise a treasure chest. Within every person, there is a treasure chest of specific talents, gifts and abilities. They are discovered by digging deep, where they are waiting to be unlocked and shared with the world. This is your potential. Some people never discover their treasure chest. For others, they discover their treasure chest but never discover the keys to unlocking it to realise their potential.

Discovering the keys allows you to take control of your future, to dream with confidence, and opens up future possibilities while at school and beyond, which is motivating. It brings hope and provides a sense of freedom to know that success isn't automatically handed to the super talented, but to those who discover the keys to unlocking those gifts and abilities.

You're not entitled to success – you earn it. You'll not only gain a deeper understanding of the person you are now, but also the person you can be, filling you with energy, excitement and enthusiasm. You will attract greater opportunities that will allow you to grow and discover your true purpose.

In the parable of the talents (Matthew 25:14-30), Jesus shares the importance of people using their talents that they've been entrusted with by God. Everyone has their special set. If these talents are not discovered and used, they go to waste. In other words, what you don't discover and use, you lose.

If you do not discover the keys, you're settling for less than you're capable of. You're allowing your future to be determined by what life hands to you, rather than creating your destiny with the gifts you've been given. It's easier to doubt yourself, to become lost, confused and unmotivated. As a result, you lose control and belief in your ability to achieve, igniting feelings of inadequacy, fear and anxiety. You'll never discover the person you can be and the greatness that lies within you.

After eighteen months of depression, alcohol and drugs, Nathan was sitting at home one day, reflecting on past achievements prior to his shoulder injury. In that moment of reflection and joy, flashbacks emerged of people saying that he was something special, that he could have been anything he wanted to be, that he had the whole world at his feet, and that he was the best player they'd ever seen. It reminded him of how much talent he really had. He didn't want to be one of those 'could have', 'should have' or 'would have' talents that never realised their true potential.

Digging deep, Nathan never doubted his ability, for he knew what he was capable of once he became fit, and reminded himself that the real Nathan is one of the best talents in Australia. Nathan began dreaming again, igniting a driving force within him to turn his life around.

Nathan's main motivation was his grandmother, wanting to make her proud after being deeply hurt from seeing the look of disgust on her face while on that addictive and destructive path. He dreamed of buying her a new home, and to do so, he knew that professional Rugby League would financially allow him to turn this dream into reality within a short space of time.

Nathan aspired to achieve what his older brother didn't, bringing his late mother's vision and belief to reality. While just as talented, Nathan's brother was told by their late mother that he had the potential to play professional rugby league, but he was severely impacted after her death and turned to alcohol, leading to wasted potential.

Nathan wanted to be a role model to young people in his community, not wanting them to grow up around drugs and alcohol like he experienced, and to give them hope that there was more to life than drugs and alcohol, and that hard work does pay off.

Armed with a driving force at seventeen, Nathan secured a job at the National Parks, keeping him busy in something he was passionate about. Working on land, putting out fires, controlling pests – these all contributed to helping him get back on his feet and away from the toxic environment of alcohol and drugs.

Within months after deciding to turn his life around, Nathan was invited to a training trial with a leading NRL team. Having not played in two years, Nathan grabbed the opportunity, went down, worked hard and gave it his best shot, knowing that his dream depended on it. Witnessing his ability first hand, the club signed him on a two-year contract within days, giving him another chance to unlock the truth of his potential.

For the remaining parts of this chapter, I will share three keys to unlocking the truth of your potential in school and in life.

1) A DRIVING FORCE

"There is a powerful driving force inside every human being that once unleashed can make any vision, dream or desire a reality."
— Anthony Robbins

At sixteen, a powerful driving force within me was ignited, and I decided to take control and turn my life around and make my final year of school count. Three things motivated me.

First: to prove people wrong. For most of primary and high school, my self-belief was damaged by the graffiti of negative labels – from bullies, peers and several teachers. It held me back for many years, but turning the pain from the footy field experience into fuel empowered me to move forward.

Second: to make my parents proud. They were the only people who ever really had my back. Because they were working-class immigrants, they sacrificed everything to provide for their children.

Third: to be somebody that I can be proud of – to be my own best friend.

"The starting point of all achievement is desire."
— Napoleon Hill

Dreams are powerful, yet very personal. They allow you to visualise possibilities. They are not reserved for the special few, but are free and available for all. Your dreams provide a true reflection of who you are and your deepest desires, independent of what other people think.

In finding your driving force, ponder these three questions:

1. What motivates you?
2. Are they strong reasons to succeed?
3. What have been your greatest achievements in life to date?

Break up your dreams into categories, such as personal, family, career, relationships, financial, health, experiences and contribution.

Examples of dreams include:

- making your parents proud
- proving people wrong
- acing your school exams
- making it into the representative team for your sport
- gaining positive recognition
- getting out of your comfort zone and trying new things
- getting a part time job while at school
- becoming the person/leader/sportsman/artist you aspire to be
- going on the career path you'd like to pursue
- gaining the income you'd like to earn and living your ideal lifestyle
- having the friends you'd like to have
- having the ideal partner you'd like to share life with
- having the health you'd like to enjoy
- living the experiences you'd like
- making the contribution you'd like to make

How important are your dreams to you?
Importance breeds commitment, which leads to action. Internalise the feelings of achieving your dreams and the impact on your loved ones. What will it mean for you if those dreams come true? What will it mean to the people around you? Your loved ones? To the world? To your own world?

Consider the type of impact you can make by achieving

your dreams. This will inspire you and add fuel to your drive. When times get tough, your driving force becomes your light, a source of hope and something to believe in.

2) A PATH

"Opportunity doesn't knock, it presents itself when you beat the door down."
— Kyle Chandler

Determining your pathway is about taking responsibility and ownership for your future. It's important to be curious, and to step out and explore these pathway options before finishing school, because that is where you will find opportunities.

This allows you to not only envision what's possible after school, but also the steps you need to take now to turn your dreams into reality and to realise your potential. By doing this, you get clarity and energy, and it will alleviate the stress and anxiety that arise from the fear of the unknown.

Your strengths and passions are the key in determining the best pathway for you once you leave school. It's the pathway that you will enjoy and excel most at, and your choices should reflect this.

The most commonly pursued pathways by young people are as follows:

1. Tertiary studies
2. Vocational Education and Training (VET)
3. Straight into the workforce (retail, admin, family business)

4. GAP year
5. Army
6. Starting a business

For Year 10 students, the subject electives you choose for your senior years pave the path for what courses you may be able to be admitted into, not only based on the entry result, but also on prerequisites as well. For people who want to pursue careers in areas such as law, finance, medicine or engineering, then tertiary studies is the ideal path.

Perhaps you don't see yourself going down the tertiary path and are more interested in taking up a trade. The VET path comprises of opportunities to do an apprenticeship or a combined work and study program. Examples of apprenticeships include plumbing, electrical, carpentry, building and hairdressing.

Seek guidance by speaking to teachers, career advisors and even adults who are currently working in the pathway you are considering. Go out and attend career exhibitions. Conduct online research and try to get work experience in that field.

> *Whilst a successful career in professional Rugby League is his primary career pathway, Nathan's experiences taught him that the privilege to play could be taken away at any time by injury. After considering his options, Nathan created a backup pathway by completing his Certificate IV in Teacher's Aid so he could help young indigenous kids.*

Two common fears that teens experience when choosing a pathway is the fear of failure, and the fear of parent disapproval.

Fear of failure
Let's say you'd like to study a particular course at university. It's your choice, not your parents', teachers' or friends'.

What's the worst that can happen? The path is not set in stone so you can always change. Despite incurring course fees, do not see this as a negative or sign of failure. In life, there is always a price to pay on the road to success. That price could be financial, emotional, and even time. Things don't always work out at first attempt. Sometimes, we are meant to go through certain experiences purely to grow and learn valuable lessons about life and ourselves.

Fear of parent disapproval

The fear of parent disapproval stems from the human need and desire to be loved, accepted and respected. Choosing to follow an unconventional path threatens this. Many people I know, who from the love, care, and 'unintentional' pressure from their parents, followed a path that they did not have their heart set on. The result? In most cases, they quitted before completing, not only incurring an emotional cost from the act of quitting, but also the financial cost of starting something and not finishing it.

Have you ever thought about why your parents want you to pursue one path while your heart is set on another?
Let's say you'd like to become a professional musician. It's always been your dream, but your parents want you to study law. How do you win parental support to become a professional musician?

Simply, you need to prove your commitment, passion and drive by providing evidence of the steps you are taking to turn that dream into reality. Are you practising your instrument every day? Are you taking lessons regularly? If your parents are not willing to pay for these lessons, are you prepared to get a job, to earn an income to pay for these lessons that will take you closer to your dream? When your parents see this evidence of how driven you are, they will be more inclined to support you, not stop you.

When there is understanding and evidence, there is confidence and acceptance. Deep down, your parents only want the best for you and when you can show them the reasons why you want to pursue your selected path and your commitment, you'll be in a better position to secure their support. They'll feel a sense of eternal peace of mind, supporting their child's happiness, emotional security and fulfilment.

If your parents still do not approve, seek to engage another caring adult to guide you and to be a mediator between you and your parents. It takes courage and strength to deviate from the norm. This is part of becoming your own person, making your own decisions and being willing to accept responsibility.

Be fearless in the pursuit of what sets your heart on fire, because this will not only make an impact on your life and the life of your immediate family, but also on your own family in years to come.

3) A GROWING MIND

"Continuous effort – not strength or intelligence – is the key to unlocking our potential."
— Winston Churchill

Think back over your school journey to date. Was there a student in your year that always seemed to make the school headlines of achievements? Did you ever say to yourself, 'Oh they're so talented'?

When I was in primary school, Damien always topped the class and was the fastest runner across all ages. He was tall and strong, compared to other students. I recall looking up to him in admiration, wanting to be like him. During high school, his standards dropped in both his studies and athletics. He was distracted and not driven. Damien finished high school with an average result in his final exams.

Was Damien talented? Absolutely. However, the problem was he relied on his talent alone to achieve and maintain success, yet that talent only got him so far. He had plenty of opportunities to unlock his potential, but lacked a driving force, and didn't put the effort in. There are many talented individuals like Damien who do not unlock their full potential because of their attitude and mindset towards success.

Carol Dweck, author of *Mindset: The New Psychology of Success*, states that a person can adopt one of two mindsets in life: a **fixed mindset** or a **growth mindset**. Each has a view on how success is achieved and is a measurement of one's true potential.

The **fixed mindset** believes that talent, intelligence, personality and character are set in stone. You're either naturally smart or not. This mindset does not believe in effort and a person's potential is *limited*.

The **growth mindset** believes that talent, intelligence, personality and character are developed through consistent effort, self belief, and perseverance. This mindset believes effort is the mother of growth, and that a person's potential is *unlimited*.

The difference between the two is belief.

Do you believe that success is only reserved for those who are talented, gifted and smart?
Talent is overrated. One of my mentors once said that the distraction factor for talented people is extremely high, implying that no matter how talented a person is, if they do not continue to work on improving what they have, they will not achieve. Don't be fooled by the myth of talent.

> _Though super talented, Nathan realised if he kept relying on talent, he would remain playing Rugby League back at home, and that's as far as he would go. Playing at the highest level in the NRL required Nathan to not only adopt a growth mindset where he continually worked hard on his skills, speed, and mental toughness, but also constantly surrounded himself with a positive support network to maintain strong mental health in order to avoid the negative emotions, associations and addictive behaviours that sent him on a downward spiral at sixteen._

I was never one of those students who could rock up to an exam without studying and top the class, so I never felt I had natural talents that I could rely on. I wasn't great at sport, and my academic results up until the end of Year 11 were average, with some subjects not even making a pass. For most of my school life, I had a fixed mindset belief in that being 'smart' was just a natural thing.

So how did I go from an average student in Year 11 to finishing in the top 10% of Australia by the conclusion of Year 12?

It didn't happen overnight.

My self-belief had been battered over many years, so to move forward, I had to rebuild it. I decided to start afresh, to look forward, and to not allow my past results and experiences to dictate what was possible for me in the future.

Effort was something that I had control over, so I chose to apply myself and use effort as the tool to build my belief.

I became more attentive in class. I didn't leave assignments to the last minute. I kept a good set of notes and prepared well for exams. I would spend lunch times and free periods studying in the library. Some days, I would stay back after school to seek help from teachers. For subjects I struggled with, I decided to get good at them by asking questions and seeking support from teachers. I discovered that if I could learn one thing, I could learn many things.

Every day, I fed the good wolf with inspirational music and positive affirmations, powering my driving force, especially during stressful times, such as leading into exams, meeting due dates for assessments, and overall fatigue.

Over time, I saw progress, building my belief. With self-belief, consistent effort and perseverance, I grew not only intellectually, but also, more importantly, emotionally. Adopting the growth mindset was the catalyst for my transformation and achievements in school and life thereafter.

Having never spoken in public until my mid twenties, I was not a naturally gifted communicator who could get up in front of people and speak effortlessly. When I had the desire to become a professional speaker, it was the growth mindset that created the possibility, and consistent effort allowed me to develop the skills, belief and resilience to turn my dream into reality.

The growth mindset allowed me to discover the truth of my potential – as a teen and an adult – and that truth being that my potential was unlimited.

Do you have a fixed or growth mindset?
Consider these questions:

- Are you allowing your past results to dictate what's possible for you in the future?
- Are you one who believes that success is only reserved for the talented, gifted and smart people?
- Are you prepared to put in the effort and persevere in order to achieve?

Over the years, I've come to realise that the greatest asset that a person could possess is the growth mindset. Self-belief became the oxygen for hope and possibility in my life, and the key to unlocking my potential.

It's possible for you too. Your past doesn't have to be your future. It's never too late to grow with the growth mindset and unlock the truth of your potential.

EXERCISE

Complete the following:

- Write down a list of ninety-nine dreams, including one where you choose three people that you would like to make proud. Reflect on the examples shared earlier to assist with your dream building. Even the smallest things like buying a pair of your favourite shoes or shouting your whole family dinner at the Sheraton Hotel are dreams and should be listed.
- For the strengths, passions and interests that you identified when completing the S.T.U.F.F analysis, make a list showing how they can be turned into opportunities and potential career pathways. (e.g. Strength = Creativity | Opportunity = Graphic Designer)
- To build your self-belief and set you on a growth

mindset path, write down a list of specific things that you can do to exercise greater effort in your studies, sport and extracurricular activities.

SUMMARY

1. It's one thing to have potential, and everyone has it, both known or unknown. It's another thing to unlock this potential. A driving force, a pathway and a growing mind will enable you to unlock and discover the truth of your potential

2. Everyone has a special set of talents, skills and abilities – and what you don't use, you lose.

3. Choose a post-school pathway based on your strengths and passions. It's the pathway that you will enjoy and excel most at. If it's different to the path that your parents have in mind, show the evidence to your parents of how driven you are towards your dream to win their approval.

5. WINNING INGREDIENTS

"Some people want it to happen, some wish it would happen, others make it happen."
— Michael Jordan

When Billy was eight, he first hit a golf ball during a day out with his father. At sixteen, he had his eyes set on becoming a professional golfer, hoping to represent Australia at the PGA tour.

Like other teens living in the digital age, Billy has many distractions around him. Despite this, he has been able to maintain a laser-like focus to successfully balance both school and sporting commitments, and to be at the top of his game in both, achieving outstanding results.

Billy is not special, nor is he a natural talent. He has just applied the same recipe for success as other high achievers.

Success is not a fluke.

Just like the making of a delicious cake relies on a winning recipe, so too does achieving success in school and in life.

Winning ingredients create a pathway for high achievement of clarity, belief and focus, enabling you to fight off anything negative, such as procrastination, distractions and obstacles. While many teens are consumed by social media, winning ingredients will give you strength and discipline to overcome these temptations and to stay on course as you take greater control and responsibility of your life.

They also build your emotional muscles when it comes to work ethic. You develop the mental toughness to accept the challenge that comes from pursuing the dream, because it creates excitement and growth, and stretches you as a person. That winning attitude will serve you in many years to come with anything that you pursue. If you've done it once, you can do it again.

When you don't know where you are going, it's easy to drift off and waste time, be drawn into the wrong social group, and be prone to addictive behaviour. Without the winning ingredients, you lose control of the steering wheel.

By losing control, you won't be able to find out what you are truly capable of because you have chosen to settle for mediocre results. This limits not only your opportunities when you leave school, but also the type of character that you're taking into the next chapter of your life.

Fear, stress and anxiety emerge when there is uncertainty. Walking into an unknown future with no clear direction or purpose can have a ripple effect on multiple areas of your life, not only your learning experience, growth and results at school, but also your future career prospects, income potential, personal relationships and quality of life.

Success leaves clues.

Whether you aspire to achieve high school grades, play representative sport, become an artist, doctor, builder, personal trainer or business entrepreneur, neither talent nor luck alone can bring this dream into reality. The winning ingredients will.

For the remaining parts of this chapter, I will share the five winning ingredients that can become your recipe for success in school and in life.

1) GET A GOAL

"You can't hit a target you cannot see, and you cannot hit a target you do not have."
— Zig Ziglar

Dreams are not goals. They may motivate you, but a dream alone is not enough to achieve success.

Billy is crystal clear about his overarching future goal: to be a professional golfer. He also has other career aspirations that he is working towards. His goals are written down and always in sight for constant reminders and motivation. Billy also sets daily goals, which he found to be highly effective in making every day count, because it allows him to tick off all achievements for each day and feel accomplished knowing that the day wasn't wasted and is one step closer towards achievement.

Billy's goals inspire him to go that one step further beyond the demands of teachers, coaches and peers, and is motivated by the satisfaction of being challenged and stretched as well as the fear of being average.

"Goals are only important if they win games."
— Lionel Messi

Defined, written-down goals win games. Research has shown that there's so much power in written-down goals.

Growing up, Dasni had many challenges. Diagnosed with leukemia in primary school, her parents moved her to a new school during Year 7, and upon arrival she became a target for bullying and social exclusion. At seventeen, she lost vision in her left eye. Despite this, it didn't stop Dasni's determination to pursue her dream to become a psychologist and help children.

In her final school year, Dasni drew a gigantic 98 and placed it in front of her desk to remind her every day to keep focussed. Due to her medical condition, she found it difficult to maintain focus from constantly having to treat her vision with eye drops. At times when Dasni could barely see, she relied on her parents to read study notes to her, and pushed herself to learn and memorise, rather than give excuses.

Despite her physical handicap, it didn't stop Dasni from consistently visualising the end result in her mind. She followed through on the advice from Dory in Finding Nemo: "When life gets tough, do you wanna know what you gotta do? Just keep swimming."

Dasni just kept swimming. Fast forward a few years, after having achieved her goals, Dasni is living her dream and helping children.

2) GET A PLAN

Have you ever felt so overwhelmed and stressed by the amount of school work staring back at you? Did you think there's just not enough time? There is just not enough time to do everything, but there is always enough time to do the most important things.

You can't manage time. It's fixed. Everyone has twenty-four hours each day. The only thing you can manage are your priorities.

Imagine an ordinary jar. The jar represents your time. Next, imagine the jar is filled with rocks, representing the really important stuff, like studies, family, well-being and faith. The jar is still not full. Next, the pebbles are poured into the jar. They represent the semi-important stuff like social outings, friends and relationships. Despite the jar filled with rocks and pebbles, the jar is still not full. The jar is then filled with sand, representing the non-important things, such as social media, internet browsing, excess TV watching and gossiping.

Here's the key: if all that remained in the jar were the rocks, the important stuff still would get done. But if you fill the jar with pebbles and sand first, there would be no room for the rocks.

Are you allocating time towards your rocks? Are you scheduling your study commitments to avoid stress and cramming?

> *Leading into her final school year, Anita felt she had a balanced life. She had a good circle of friends, a great family life, competed at a local level in swimming, and studied when she needed to.*
>
> *When experiencing stress midway through the first term by the amount of work she had to do, Anita knew something had to change.*
>
> *She began to prioritise her rocks – her study commitments, especially leading into exams. Between Monday and Friday, she allocated time in her diary to study for each subject as well as scheduling two days a week for swimming. She also made time on weekends to spend with family and friends as a break once her study was done.*
>
> *In the lead-up to exams, Anita referred to the exam timetable when choosing what subjects to study for and on what date, prioritising subjects depending on which exam came first. This significantly reduced her stress levels. She also stopped swimming temporarily during her final exams so she wasn't overwhelmed. Two weeks prior to her final exams, she stayed at her uncle's place to be in a distraction-free environment. All these changes improved Anita's emotional state and lead to her success in her final exams.*

"If you fail to plan, you plan to fail."
— Benjamin Franklin

Getting organised and designing a plan allows you to take action on the defined goals that you have set.

> *Billy uses a printout timetable to plan and schedule his study and sporting commitments to keep him organised. He is diligent about ensuring all drills are completed by the end of each day.*

Is there structure in your game plan or are you just drifting and wondering, hoping to travel in the right direction? Lack of structure breeds confusion, doubt and fear.

Whilst the final years of school can be stressful, they can also be fun, with many opportunities to have fun from social experiences. There is a time to do these things, but rather than jump on every opportunity to have fun, I would recommend allocating these social activities to your leisure time and not the time you've allocated towards working towards your goals. You need to be selective, and sacrifice is required.

> *While completing Year 12, Raj's dear friend, Tom, was found shot dead at point blank at the door step of his home. It rocked Raj's world, making him realise how short life was. For most of his school life, Raj was just going with the flow with no real goals or direction, as well as hanging around with the wrong people.*

> *After Tom's death, Raj decided to not waste another day of school and life. It was challenging for Raj, given he had Attention Deficit Hyperactivity Disorder (ADHD) and was easily prone to daydreaming and distractions. To overcome this, Raj pre-planned his days into hourly slots using a simple spreadsheet, and filled these slots with his study commitments. At the end of each day, he would write on a piece of paper all the things achieved that day. He also found that music helped increase his focus, as it blocked out the noise and distractions at home. Now, Raj is building a successful career in law.*

3) GET LASER-FOCUSSED

"The successful warrior is the average man, with laser-like focus."
— Bruce Lee

A laser-like focus requires you to work in time blocks, while logged out and in an empowering environment.

Billy studies in ninety-minute blocks of time, ensuring his desk is clear each time to enhance concentration. He also likes to change the environment so it doesn't get boring. As a daily routine, he arrives to school early to spend some time in the library revising his homework before the school day begins.

Billy limits his time on social media to two hours a week, after seeing the harmful effects that excess usage has had on his peers, who are constantly distracted and falling behind in their studies.

Treat your time blocks as sacred – no distractions. Focus on one thing only. Give yourself a time goal for each task and put a timer next to you so you can stay focussed with a sense of urgency.

Eliminate weapons of mass distraction, like social media and text messaging. For example, temporarily log out of your social media accounts so notifications don't keep popping up. You can always log back in. Keep your phone on silent and in your bag to avoid seeing flashes popping up. It's all about personal momentum and delving deep into the zone to maximise your learning experience. Remember, your mind is like any other muscle that requires training to become stronger.

Ensure you keep healthy snacks and water next to you to maintain energy, and to remove the urge to get up and become distracted.

An empowering environment around you not only enhances your ability to focus, but also provides that positive reminder of why you were doing what you were doing.

For example, having your goals in sight, whether it's on the wall, door or computer is extremely powerful, as well as posting motivational messages and positive images in your study or training space that fuel and energise you. For some people, playing relaxing instrumental music in the background enhances their concentration by helping them zone into their studies. Everyone is different. Apply what works for you.

If you're finding it difficult to focus, either due to distractions or procrastinating, set small goals with a deadline. The deadline will force you to avoid procrastination. Always be reminded of how important your goals are to you. If they are important to you, you will find a way. If not, then you will make excuses.

If you have distractions at home that you cannot control, find an alternative place to study. It could be the library, community centre, park (before it gets cool and dark) or even a quiet café. Where there is a will, there is a way.

It's easy to focus when doing things you enjoy but there will be occasions where you'll feel unmotivated to do the things you don't enjoy, like an assignment, an exam and training drills. Thoughts may run through your mind like, 'I won't need this in the future', 'How does this apply to me', 'I can't be bothered', and 'I'm not academic; I don't give a stuff.'

"You have to do what you have to do so you can do
what you want to do."
— Josh Shipp

For example, what do you do when you hate a subject? It comes back to your attitude. In life, sometimes you have options, sometimes you don't. There will be many occasions where you're required to do things you don't like, but the value you receive from that experience is dependent on your attitude and approach to it. There is always something to learn, whether it is relating to doing things that you enjoy and do not enjoy.

For the things you don't enjoy, motivation comes from getting into action mode, even on days where you may feel unmotivated to do anything. Those days will come, and when motivation doesn't come direct to you like a pizza delivery, you can create it by getting stuck into doing what you need to do. Whether it's studying, going for a run or cleaning your bedroom, when you see progress and what you have achieved when you didn't feel like doing it, that is motivating.

As with the karate analogy, it's about focussing through the brick, not on the brick, and what's beyond what it is that you don't like.

4) GET CONNECTED

Not all subjects were Billy's favourites, and he lost focus in subjects he did not enjoy. To overcome this, asking questions and seeking advice from teachers enabled him to understand, engage in and enjoy the learning, rather than endure it. He found that studying with a small group kept him focussed, as each person is feeding off each other and keeping the other motivated.

No one becomes successful on their own. Your success can be fast-tracked by seeking support from teachers, tutors and coaches, and even your parents, siblings and peers. It's about building relationships and trust. There's the saying, 'When the student is ready, the teacher appears.' You need to show initiative. Asking for help is a sign of strength, not weakness, and a display of commitment and desire to learn and grow.

Despite being voted the world's best football player multiple times, Cristiano Ronaldo still uses a coach to maintain peak performance.

A coach or mentor will help you improve and stay on course. For example, when you may experience a drop in focus because you don't see progress in a particular area, having regular check-ins with your mentor not only keeps you accountable, but also can show the progress you are making. From their experience, they can see things that perhaps you can't. Having that access to support will help you develop your skills and techniques in the area which you are working towards excelling at.

5) GET OVER IT

"It's hard to beat a person who never gives up."
— Babe Ruth

On many occasions during Year 12, my will to win was tested.

Motivation was not always high. There were subjects I didn't enjoy and there were subjects that I really struggled with that gave me anxiety, especially leading into exams.

I would often hear an inner voice whisper things like, 'Why are you studying so hard?', 'You're not making any progress,' and 'Have fun like everyone else. It's your last year of school.'

Despite this, I kept going, embracing the grind. I cut out all distractions, especially technology and negative social influences. I kept reciting, "Short-term pain, for long-term gain. I'll pay now to play later, rather than play now and pay later."

Whilst my results were not consistent, my effort throughout the year was because I kept reminding myself that it's a marathon, not a sprint.

During most lunch breaks, I would head straight to the library to study and I would be ridiculed by peers in passing along the way, calling me a nerd.

Though irritating, it motivated me because I was choosing to focus on my future. Nothing was going to stop me.

On your journey, your will to win will be tested too by challenges such as lack of motivation, battered belief, failure, stress and anxiety, and other situations outside of your control.

Winners triumph in spite of these challenges.

You'll be required to get over these obstacles and persevere. And it's going to take grit.

> "Grit is the passion and perseverance for very long-term goals. Grit is having stamina. Grit is sticking with your future, day in, day out, not just for the week, not just for the month, but for years, and working really hard to make that future a reality. Grit is living life like it's a marathon, not a sprint."
> — Amy Lee Duckworth

Is grit something you're born with? Absolutely not.

Just like a person's true potential is unlocked when adopting the growth mindset, grit is a product of the growth mindset, because in order to win, it requires *consistent effort, patience* and *mental toughness*.

When the going gets tough, people with grit keep going and are not crushed by setbacks. They place value in the struggle and sacrifice because that's where the growth is. The greater the struggle, the greater the fulfilment.

Do you have enough grit to stay the course?

The Chinese bamboo tree needs to be fertilised and watered every day from the moment the little seed is planted in the ground.

If you fertilise and water the seed for one year, you'll see no changes. After two years, nothing. After three years, still nothing, and by this point, your confidence may drop and you will feel like giving up. But if you keep watering and fertilising the seed consistently through the fourth year, then by the fifth year, you'll see the Chinese bamboo tree grow about 30 metres tall in six weeks.

Patience coupled with consistency and perseverance breeds hope, possibility and prosperity. Pain is temporary; it's only a short period of time.

When the going gets tough, hold to the vision to win and trust the process of effort, sacrifice and challenges. It's part of the story.

If, after reading this chapter, you still feel like it's impossible to achieve your goals, remember the words of Zig Ziglar: "Travel as far as you can go, and once you get there, you will always be able to see further."

You'll nail 100% of the shots that you don't go for. While you can't control the outcome of your efforts, you are in complete control of how much effort you do put in. Do not allow the fear of failure to hold you back from going for your goal.

Sometimes you win games, sometimes you lose, but in both scenarios, you have the opportunity to grow and become a better person because of the experiences, not the results. Self-belief grows when you grow. You'll only grow when in motion, when going after your dreams and goals and when working your butt off relentlessly.

EXERCISE

Complete the following:

- Write down one 'overarching' twelve-month goal for each category of your rocks (i.e. school, sport, family, career planning, faith, health).

  Once complete, break each overarching goal into smaller monthly, weekly and daily goals that act as building blocks to achieving the overarching goals. Ensure all goals are specific, written down, deadline-driven and measurable.

- Write down a list of things that consume your time, and break them up into rocks, pebbles and sand. With consideration to the goals you have set, create a recurring weekly plan that schedules fixed time blocks to allow you to focus on your rocks first. (I would recommend using Google Sheets so you can always have access to it.)

- Whether for studying, training or practising, describe your ideal peak performance environment, and list one thing you can do to i) beat procrastination, ii) stop your biggest distraction, and iii) take action when unmotivated.

SUMMARY

1. Success is not a fluke. There is a recipe. Remember the five *winning ingredients* that will lead you to achievement: a goal, a plan, a laser focus, support and perseverance when the going gets tough.

2. There is never enough time to do everything, but there is always enough time to do the most important things. Know your priorities.

3. Success is never a straight path. There are ups and downs. Harnessing the power of a laser-like focus will ensure you stay the course. Hold to the vision, trust the process.

6. BREAKING THE CHAINS

"There is no illusion greater than fear."
— Lao Tzu

*B*harath was raised in a traditional middle-class family in India. Like most Asian parents, they heavily promoted education. His brother was his best friend, a listening ear, and motivator, yet their parents made Bharath always feel second-best, not good enough and constantly put down.

When his brother left India after being admitted to Harvard University, things went downhill for Bharath. Not having an open channel of communication with his parents, Bharath's fears made him feel imprisoned. He was physically abused when not meeting his parents' expectations, with the pressure becoming so high that he became suicidal.

Bharath persevered until his final day of school, and then decided to leave India to start a new journey in another country on his terms. Once he reached his mid twenties, a sequence of events took place in his life that ignited feelings of blame towards his parents for the things that had happened, and for the things he missed out on as a teen.

Despite the fact the years had passed, there was lingering hurt. Bharath realised he needed closure with his parents and organised to reunite with them to have a detailed conversation. It was a healing experience for Bharath and his parents, when all realised that growing up, Bharath never really communicated what was important to him because he always lived in fear due to the cultural barriers of respect and authority.

After healing old wounds, Bharath went on to thrive in life, becoming a successful business owner of TradeShifu and achieving financial freedom at 26. Bharath's parents knew him best, and all he needed to do to remove the intense pressure experienced in his teens was to talk.

There are many teens that feel just like Bharath felt in his teens.

At some point during your school journey, you will feel the pressure to perform and the pressure to conform. It may come from parents and teachers wanting you to do well, from peers wanting you to conform, and from your own personal ambition to achieve a certain level.

This pressure gives birth to two types of fears. The first is performance fear, like the fear of failure in an exam, sporting match, job interview, on stage performance, arising from the pressure to perform. The second is social fear, and this can be the fear of disapproval, not being liked and fitting in, which arises from the pressure to conform.

Fear is a normal human emotion, but is also the mother of all monkeys.

You cannot control when it shows up, because then you'll be fighting human nature, but you do have a choice of whether you control the fear, or it controls you. Carrying unmanaged fears is like being chained, unable to move, and trapped. These emotions are part of one family, Enzo's family.

What would your life look like if you crushed all your fears, stress and anxiety?
All great achievements are on the other side of fear.

Breaking these chains will free you from unhealthy pressure, and replace the crippling emotion of fear with the empowering emotions of love, joy, happiness and personal freedom. Your relationships with your parents and teachers will be enhanced, rather than fractured. You'll grow, perform and stretch yourself beyond what you thought was possible. You'll be empowered to tackle your challenges head on, and this will boost your confidence levels, because you have taken action in something that you thought was once your worst nightmare. You'll gain back control over your emotional state, and no longer will you have to endure the pain of stress and constant worry.

If the chains aren't broken, a minor case can become major and chronic, causing serious mental health problems. High levels of stress can have negative effects on the way you study, train and prepare, resulting in an unconfident delivery and mediocre performance. It can impact your mental health, where you have constant feelings of debilitating nerves, concern and worry. It can also cause bodily reactions such as digestive problems and dermatitis, and can have a negative impact on your physical health.

For the remaining parts of this chapter, I will share three steps that will help you manage your performance fears, deal with pressure, and reduce your overall stress and anxiety levels.

These steps can be applied in any situation where you are required to perform, but for the purposes of this chapter, I will explain each step using the performance example of school exams.

STEP 1: ACKNOWLEDGE THE FEAR

When I decided to pursue my dream of becoming a professional speaker, I recall saying to myself at the time, 'Dan, are you nuts? You want to become a professional speaker? Dude, you've never spoken in public, ever. There's no way you're good enough to become a pro.'

That was my negative self-talk chatting away. It had a point. I was not good enough to become a professional right at that moment, but my positive self-talk responded back: 'I might not be good enough now, but you're not stopping me from getting good.'

I had many fears, though – the fear of going blank on stage, being judged, messing up my words, stuttering, saying the wrong thing, and losing credibility given my lack of experience. These feelings were all channelled from my fear of failure.

Despite the fears, I decided to go for it and not allow them to immobilise and cripple me. My vision and purpose was far greater than any fears I had.

Early in my speaking career, I was extremely nervous before every event, breathing heavily, my body shaking and always feeling the urge to go to the bathroom, not once, twice, but at least ten times before starting time.

It was fear, stress and anxiety that affected me. While irritating, I affirmed in my mind to push through with the knowledge that the uncomfortable becomes comfortable over time. The more I spoke in public, the more comfortable it became, and the number of times I went to the bathroom before these events dropped.

You should ask yourself these questions before every performance to tune in to your fears:

- Which fear is holding me back?

- How does the fear show up in me?

- Have I decided to run with the fear rather than try and fight it off?

Which fear is holding you back? The fear of failure, other people's opinions, the unknown, and rejection are the most common teen fears.

For example, if you're feeling constant stress and anxiety from the possibility of not doing well in an exam, resulting in letting others down, then fear of failure is holding you back.

Consider the reasons why you fear failure. Are unrealistic expectations causing you stress? If they are, then this is unhealthy pressure that needs to be managed, which I will expand more upon shortly. The fear of failure could also be caused by lack of preparation, not feeling good enough and loved, regardless of the result.

When tuning in, acknowledge the signs indicating when fear has shown up.

Since fear is an emotion and is invisible, its effects can be seen through your *body*. Nausea, heavy breathing, going blank in an exam, sweaty palms, diarrhoea, trembling, crying and hitting are all signs when fear has made its presence.

A sign that fear has popped up in your *mind* through negative self-talk is when you have the following thoughts, like 'There is no way I'll be able to get that result', 'It's too hard,' or 'That person will never go out with me.' These thoughts are confidence-crushing.

Fear can show up in some of the *choices* you make. Choosing to procrastinate rather than study for your exams, choosing to stay in your comfort zone, choosing not to choose because you are indecisive, and choosing not to attempt or complete something unless it is perfect are all signs that fear is taking effect.

Once you have acknowledged the presence of fear and its effects on you, have you made the decision to embrace and tackle it head on?

What you resist will persist. You can either choose to *run with* the fear and control how it affects your performance or you can *run from* the fear and allow it to control you.

STEP 2: ADJUST THE VOLUME

Fear is the sound of your emotions, and once you can identify the channel it is coming from, you can adjust the volume of this sound so it does not negatively affect your ability to perform. The sound of confidence needs to be raised, so the sound of fear cannot be heard.

"Confidence is preparation. Everything else is beyond your control."
– Richard Kline

The sound of confidence is increased through effective preparation. There are four key areas of preparation to focus on before any performance to ensure you deliver your personal **BEST**:

1. Body

2. Emotions

3. Schedule

4. Technique

The B.E.S.T framework can be used for any situation where one is required to perform, whether academically, in sport, on stage, in a job interview, and even for asking someone out on a date.

Body

"The higher your energy level, the more efficient your body. The more efficient your body, the better you feel and the more you will use your talent to produce outstanding results."
— Anthony Robbins

Your physical state affects your emotional state, making a difference on your energy levels.

Here are four areas to focus on:

1. **Sleep**: Make sure you get plenty of it.

   Any less than eight hours can reduce your concentration power; hence, your ability to perform. To easily transition to sleep mode every night, cease screen time at least one hour before going to bed. This will ensure you receive optimal sleep.

2. **Food**: Pay attention to the *type* and *amount* you eat.

   Eat plenty of fruits and vegetables for essential nutrients, and minimise high levels of sugar intake sourced from candy, junk food and soft drinks.

3. **Water**: Drink plenty of it and avoid caffeine and energy drinks.

   Water keeps you hydrated, energised, and suppresses your appetite so you're not always feeling hungry.

4. **Movement**: Make sure your whole body is active. Exercise ignites your energy levels, gets the blood flowing and clears the mind, becoming a great stress reliever. For example, in between time blocks of study, go for a walk and stretch. It will instantly change your physical state and you'll find it's refreshing, increasing your productivity when you return to the desk. Stress will decrease and confidence will increase when in motion.

Despite preparing well leading into exams, Anita would always feel very anxious on the day of the exam. She managed her fears by practicing a twenty-minute breathing routine using stomach muscles, clearing her mind, helping her remain calm, and allowing her brain to stay in tune and remember all the things she had learnt.

Remember, if you are feeling good on the outside, it's likely you will also feel good on the inside.

Emotions

Despite carrying a great fear of failure in Year 12, Raj was deliberate about controlling his emotional state through positive quotes and anecdotes. The following quotes helped Raj in times of doubt and stress:

- *'If you run, you stand a chance of losing, but if you don't, you've already lost.' (Barack Obama)*
- *'You gotta be able to smile through the bullshit.' (Tupac Shakur)*
- *'I hated every minute of training, but I said, don't quit. Suffer now and live the rest of your life as a champion.' (Muhammad Ali)*

He would often recite these quotes to himself before an exam or during a tense period, igniting the courage within him to drive through his fears.

How can you have an abundant flow of positive emotions leading into your next performance?
Stay plugged in to your driving force to remain powered up and motivated. Keep constant daily reminders around you.

Practise mindfulness and meditation to reconnect with yourself and be reminded of the fullness of your truth – your identity, worth and potential.

Visualise performance day and see yourself as worthy and capable, and that delivering your personal best is all that you expect of yourself, regardless of the result.

Leave the rest to your faith. Whether you believe in God or not, tapping into inner spirituality will ignite the courage you need to crush your fears.

Being the eldest child, Bethany felt the heat during Year 12 on the back of a series of events while growing up, such as her parents' separation, bullying, depression and the death of her grandmother. Thoughts of letting her parents down and being a disappointment constantly ran through her mind. She also had eczema, which interrupted her preparation and raised her fears of not doing well on exam day.

In managing her emotional state, Bethany ensured she was well prepared leading into exams, but she also used Post-it notes while studying to act as a reminder that she's prepared. This made her feel good and reduced her stress and pressure. She also had a supportive partner who gave her positive reinforcement.

Maintain open communication with your circle of support about where you are at and how you feel. Despite feeling the stress from wanting to do well, having a laugh regularly will help you to relax and not take things too seriously, while knowing there are bigger problems globally.

Schedule

"You cannot escape the responsibility of tomorrow by
evading it today."
— Abraham Lincoln

Teens feel overwhelmed when they feel that too much is on
their plate. As a result, they stress, worry and, ultimately,
procrastinate. Procrastination is just fear in disguise; and
when things are not done, it builds up stress and anxiety.

In the Winning Ingredients chapter, I mentioned the rocks,
pebbles and sand analogy. This is not only a great analogy for
priority management, but also for stress reduction. Effective
preparation comes back to knowing your priorities, and
scheduling to do them.

The number one killer of procrastination is scheduling
really small goals during your preparation. Break large,
overwhelming tasks into small bite-sized pieces to reduce
the build-up of stress and anxiety.

Breaking it up not only paves the way for immediate action,
but also, by biting away piece by piece, increases your
confidence levels when you see consistent progress.

Whenever you feel stressed and overwhelmed by your
workload, think of the *watermelon principle*. How do you eat
a watermelon? One slice and bite at a time. Your bites are
your confidence boosters. You'll no longer need to cram and
stress yourself out.

"Happiness = Reality – Expectation."
— Tom Magliozzi

There are things in life that you can't avoid, but can only manage. One of these things is pressure.

Parents, as loving as they are, can be unintentionally annoying and pressuring. Sometimes it's healthy pressure, based on realistic expectations, which can ignite positive emotions, and encourage and motivate you, despite the fear of failure at the back of your mind.

Other times, it's unhealthy pressure, which is based on unrealistic expectations. These can ignite negative emotions, such as stress and anxiety, due to the overwhelming fear of failure in the front of your mind, as seen in Bharath's story.

It's common at your age that open communication with parents is at its lowest, because you are seeking your own independence and social approval.

Dealing with unhealthy pressure is about knowing yourself and building positive relationships with your parents and teachers, so the expectation gap is closed. This won't happen unless you schedule the time to do it.

Everyone has different strengths and abilities. The truth is you can't be good at everything. For example, if your parents expect you to score a grade of 90% in Maths, but you know that it's not your strongest subject. You're more confident in English. You need to talk about it and perhaps set a more realistic goal.

Communication feeds understanding and builds trust. Don't keep it inside, because that will build unhealthy pressure and lead to a setup for failure. Build empathy by trading places with your parents and ask yourself, 'If I had a son or daughter like me, what would I expect of them?'

If you find that your parents are irrational, overbearing and placing unhealthy pressure on you, ensure that you have built good relationships with your teachers so they can support you. No parent wants other than the best for their child.

Focus on what's in your control – your effort, not results. Giving your best shot is the only expectation you should allow yourself to carry.

"A diamond is chunk of coal that did well under pressure."
— Henry Kissinger

Technique

Consider these scenarios: Rugby league superstar Johnathan Thurston about to take the goal kick to secure an additional two points for his team; Lionel Messi about to take the free kick for FC Barcelona; Roger Federer about to take a serve in Wimbledon; and Adele about to reach the high notes when performing live. What are the chances of each of them 'nailing it' if it was their very first time?

Each would have rehearsed many times to strengthen their technique, because without technique, the chances of 'nailing it' are futile. Visualisation techniques and skills coaching raise the sound of confidence in their minds. They still may have fears, but will not be crippled by them.

How can you apply this to your exam preparations to develop a supreme knowledge of your game, and be filled with confidence?

"Practice doesn't make perfect. Only perfect practice does."
— Vince Lombardi

Effective studying and exam preparation involves rehearsing. This can be through practising on past exam papers, or anticipating the questions that might be asked.

You'll feel comfortable knowing that the exam day won't be the first time going through the process. You're controlling the exam situation rather than hoping, praying and being surprised. Just like a sports team or a musical band needs to train before the big day, the same applies here.

Heading into every performance, Billy knows that there will always be a degree of stress and nerves. He manages these emotions by ensuring that his studies have covered all areas that will be assessed in order to not arrive on exam day feeling unprepared and shocked.

For both exams and golf tournaments, Billy has a consistent ritual of waking up at the same time and arriving an hour and a half before start time, reducing game day stress and nerves.

Seek guidance from teachers to refine your technique. You'll become more confident as a result. A key reason for excelling in Year 12 was from an essay writing formula that my legal studies teacher shared with me at the start of Year 12, which boosted my confidence and gave me certainty towards my study and exam approach.

Had I not sought technique guidance, I would have walked into exams with much greater fear and doubt.

Everyone has a different method of study that works for them. Some people just read notes, others write them out; some type them, and others read them out loud. Do what works for you and develop a rhythm in how you undergo and learn your game.

STEP 3: ACTION, ACTION

It's time to perform!

You've prepared well, and the sound of confidence is loud, but you can still hear the whispering sound of fear that you're not going to do well. Shut that sound up and put everything in perspective by asking yourself what's the worst that can happen. Is this life or death?

"Feel the fear and do it anyway."
— Susan Jeffers

Nike yourself up and *'just do it'*.

Once you do, you'll discover that the fear was not as bad as your mind made it out to be. It was just False Evidence Appearing Real, the great acronym for fear.

EXERCISE

Complete the following:

- Write down three specific fears that are currently holding you back in school or life. Describe how the fear shows up and the impact it has on your life. Examples of specific upcoming fears include:
  - the fear of failure in the English exam
  - the fear of stuffing up of an on-stage musical performance
  - the fear of not doing well in a job interview
- In dealing with pressure to perform connected to the above fears, identify:
  - the source of pressure (e.g. external or internal)
  - the type of pressure (e.g. healthy or unhealthy)
  - one action you can do to open communication channels and discussions with parents and teachers to reduce this pressure.
- For the three fears mentioned above, use the B.E.S.T framework and write one action you can do for each component to increase your confidence and enhance your performance-related preparation, and reduce your fear, stress and anxiety. (e.g. Body = jogging, breathing exercises; Emotions = listen to music, meditation)

SUMMARY

1. Fear is a normal, human emotion. You cannot control when it shows up, but you can either choose to control it, or allow it to control you. All great achievements are on the other side of fear.

2. There are three steps to manage performance fears and deal with pressure. First, acknowledge, understand and embrace the fear. Then, adjust the volume of fear by raising the sound of confidence through effective preparation. Finally, action, action.

3. To raise the sound of confidence, the B.E.S.T preparation framework covers four areas to focus on before any performance: Body, Emotions, Schedule and Technique.

7. FREEDOM

"Before you can break out of prison, you must first realise you're locked up."
— Anonymous

In the early 1980s when North Vietnam decided to invade the south, Trung and his family – which comprised eleven adults and two children – were forced to escape in search for a better life.

With Trung's mother still pregnant with him, the family jumped on a six-foot tiny boat and headed to Thailand. Along the way, they were attacked by pirates, who luckily only took their valuables and allowed them to continue their journey.

Shortly after arriving in Thailand, Trung was born in a refugee camp. For two years, he was constantly malnourished, lacked sufficient medical attention, and was exposed to extreme poverty, disease and sickness. At times, Trung almost died from starvation.

Barely surviving that experience, the family received their lucky break to start a new life in Australia. Smelling freedom on arrival, they were placed in a detention centre for one year, before moving into a two bedroom townhouse in a Sydney suburb called Cabramatta, where most Vietnamese refugees were settled at the time.

Growing up, Trung rarely saw his parents, as they worked extremely hard just to put food on the table and make ends meet. Feeling lonely and insecure, Trung filled most of his time on the streets of Cabramatta with other refugee kids and became easily influenced by their behaviours. It was during a time when Cabramatta became known as the heroin drug capital of Australia, creating a huge opportunity for poverty-stricken refugees to make money through drug dealing.

Due to cultural and educational barriers growing up, Trung struggled to fit in and constantly felt he was not educated and worthy enough. It led him to seek further refuge by joining a notorious Vietnamese gang, and he was drawn into drugs, crime and gang warfare at a very young age.

Cabramatta train station became the prime drug hub, flooded with hundreds of dealers and users every day in a black market economy of drugs and gangland crime. Just like fellow gang members, Trung became addicted to marijuana, ecstasy, speed, alcohol and heroin. By sixteen, Trung had witnessed friends die right before his eyes from overdosing, and those who survived became 'monster' junkies or locked up in prison.

Constantly paranoid about the law and other gangs, Trung would often experience panic attacks, and be under the influence of drugs daily, tripping out and almost losing his mind and sanity completely.

Feeling locked up, Trung's addiction to drugs and gang crime was taking over his life. He wanted to escape, but didn't know how.

When it comes to any type of addiction, there is a great deal to learn from Trung's story.

Simply defined, addiction is the condition of having a *dependency, craving* or *obsession* for a substance or activity that is *pleasurable* and *repeated*, despite the substantial harm and interference it can cause with everyday life.

There are *substance abuse-type* addictions like drugs, alcohol and tobacco, and *compulsive activity-type* addictions like gaming, overeating, gambling, work, pornography, shopping, toxic relationships, and internet usage, in particular social media (SM).

This chapter will explore SM addiction. While it is not officially classified as a mental illness, it has many similarities to drug and alcohol addiction, which are classified as a mental illness.

Breaking free from SM addiction will allow you to take back control of your life, your time and your emotional state, and relationships. You'll develop greater interpersonal skills that will strengthen your existing offline relationships, enabling you to feel greater connection, meaning and intimacy to experience real joy and happiness

You'll develop greater social skills and confidence in new interactions with others, creating the opportunity to develop new meaningful offline relationships.

You'll also develop greater life skills from engaging with different people in different places, in different situations, and learning opportunities to develop new perspectives and build your emotional intelligence and resilience.

Breaking free will enhance your performance and experience level, and enable you to develop greater focus and presence in every aspect of your life – school work, communication with family and friends, new social interactions, travel, adventure, and your own personal journey of self-discovery.

Not having the urge to jump onto your newsfeed at every opportunity creates more time and personal freedom for you to exercise self-reflection, to remove the dependency on seeking attention, and the likes and validation from mostly people who are not within your inner circle of loved ones.

SM addiction experts have found that the constant connection to technology can leave people feeling more alone. People are forgetting to talk to each other, and, instead, are developing intimate relationships with a robot – their smartphones.

Constant dependency to jump online to feel connected creates greater levels of emotional instability and social anxiety. It's also very brain-fatiguing and easy to be misled into believing that friends' lists and followers reflect your level of importance and value.

Without the interpersonal, social and life skills, you'll

struggle to deal with the stresses of life and solve problems effectively, and become more likely to turn to the online world to self-medicate to numb the pain, without fully addressing the core issues. Research reveals that spending excessive amounts of time on SM can lead to depression. On the flipside, depression has also been found to be a main reason why people spend hours online in the first place, especially if the depression was caused by loneliness. It's during these times when filters are used to cover up the battle being fought behind closed doors.

If you do not break free from internet addiction, you'll never truly live life to the fullest, and many things will be lost along the way like great conversations, time, sleep, playful and fun experiences, and the opportunity to discover the fullness of your truth and deliver your personal best in school and life.

RAT PARK

In the late 1970s, a famous study into drug addiction called 'Rat Park' was conducted by Canadian psychologist Bruce Alexander. It was set up to challenge the theory at the time that addiction was caused by the chemicals contained in the drugs being taken.

Prior to Rat Park, experiments were conducted where rats were placed in a cage alone, with two separate points of drinking water. One contains tap water only, and the other contains drugged water. In almost all cases, the rat gets hooked on the drugged water, consuming it till its death.

Alexander changed the experiment slightly so the rats were in a different environment to that of a small cage. He created Rat Park, a dream destination for rats, filled with plenty of food, activities and space for hanging out and connecting with other rats. The tap water and drugged water remained available for the rats to consume.

Results showed that rats in Rat Park consumed significantly less drugged water than the caged rats. With nothing to do and no one to connect with, the isolated caged rats became addicted.

The Rat Park experiment proved how a happy environment and social connectivity affect behaviour, and when there is a void, feelings of loneliness and emotional starvation lead to addictive behaviours aimed to fill that void.

By eighteen, Trung had hit rock bottom when a newfound friend said to him with love and care, "Trung, you can create your life and whatever you decide will become your destiny."

Deeply awakened by those words, Trung decided to open up to his mother about his issues. With pain in her heart, she said to him, "Son, you have two choices in your life right now. One: continue this life and you will end up in prison, dead or continue as a drug addict. Or two: you leave and start a whole new life."

Up until that moment, Trung never knew he had the freedom to choose, always feeling trapped, pressured and drawn in by his environment. Trung's immediate reaction was 'Where?'

When his mother mentioned she had a friend who lived in Alice Springs, he grabbed the opportunity to leave, packing his bags to head to "the desert" in Northern Australia.

The transition wasn't easy. Shortly after arriving, he felt lonely, lost and depressed, while still battling paranoia and the withdrawal symptoms of living drug-free. He also experienced a huge culture shock and was targeted with racist remarks from members of the Aboriginal-dominated town he was staying in.

Despite these challenges, several factors became instrumental in allowing Trung to immerse himself in a healthy environment that would free him from addiction.

First, Trung spent one year living with Derek, an ex-Singaporean army general. A spiritual man, Derek became a mentor to Trung, teaching discipline, morals, values and the essence of spirituality that became the detox that cleansed Trung. Derek breathed life and believed in Trung.

Secondly, Trung secured a job as a panelbeater within days of arriving to his new home, giving him a sense of purpose, a source of hope and the internal drive to succeed. It also became a healthy distraction while overcoming the side effects of drugs. Within three months, Trung landed a job with Virgin Blue as a baggage handler, being one of twelve people selected from three-hundred job applicants. For four months, he worked extremely hard in high temperature conditions before joining Qantas.

Lastly, the remoteness of Alice Springs allowed Trung to regularly self-reflect and figure himself out. Digging deep, he realised that his past involvement in drugs and gangs did not reflect his true self, but instead was something he was forced into at the time to fill an emotional void created from loneliness, poverty, insecurity and trauma. Lucky to still be alive at the time, he chose to leave Sydney because he didn't want to continue living a lie.

At nineteen, Trung joined the gym, began exercising and also started boxing. Exercise cleansed his mind and built his fitness and confidence. Boxing allowed him to release anger, channel his energy into positive results, and control the fire within by learning how to use it to motivate him in all aspects of life.

Everytime Trung tasted success, small or large, he wanted more, admitting that it was like taking drugs, except much better and healthier. As he saw positive changes in himself, he wanted to continue on that journey of personal development. He was meeting new people, developing positive relationships and receiving constant recognition, all positive reinforcement.

After leaving the addiction cage in Cabramatta at eighteen, Trung spent six years in Alice Springs, and it changed the course of his life completely. Immersing himself in a healthy environment gave him a sense of connection, freedom and purpose. He not only allowed himself to break free from his addictions, but he also discovered the fullness of his truth, to create a life of many accomplishments, including owning one of the most successful personal training businesses in NSW.

For the remaining parts of this chapter, I will share how you can determine if you have a SM addiction and unpack how you can develop a healthy relationship with SM to ensure a balance between the online and offline world. If you are not addicted, you can still use the hints and tips to avoid heading down the addiction path.

1) ARE YOU HOOKED?

Life is all about balance, right? Whether it's food, games, studying, sleeping, training, working, too much of anything is not healthy.

Social media: everyone loves it. The posts, comments, followers, photos, videos, articles, chat rooms and so forth, from family members right through to someone on the other side of the planet.

Not all internet usage is addictive. So what's considered *too much* when it comes to SM use? At what point do you draw the line between frequent use that is enjoyable, beneficial and healthy to an overly obsessive habit that is harmful, unhealthy and interfering with your everyday life?

Examples of addictive SM activity can be:

- frequently checking newsfeeds daily
- constantly checking notifications and counting likes and followers

- playing Facebook games, and spending hours on status updates
- posting the 'perfect' photo or video
- excessively commenting on and stalking other people's profiles

When usage becomes so time-consuming and interferes with your studies, sleep, family and social relationships, moment-to-moment experiences, self-reflection, and interpersonal communication, it leaves the boundaries of what is considered normal.

Dr Kimberly Young, a licensed psychologist and internationally known expert on internet addiction, created the *internet addiction test* to allow people to reflect on their habits, urges, behaviour and frequency of internet usage to determine if they are addicted.

I would highly recommend completing Dr Young's internet addiction test, found at netaddiction.com/internet-addiction-test/.

According to Young, there are five key signs of SM addiction that demonstrate obsessive and compulsive behaviour, as follows:

1. You spend a lot of time thinking about Facebook, Snapchat or Instagram and planning how to use it – always feeling the need to jump on and share for likes and comments.
2. You feel an urge to use SM more and more – it's your default option for free time activity.
3. You use SM in order to forget about personal problems – used as an escape from the real world, to reduce stress.
4. You become restless or troubled if you are prohibited from using SM, experiencing

withdrawal symptoms and anxiety from the fear of missing out.

5. You use SM so much that it has a negative impact on your relationships. You become more comfortable online than offline, and it becomes your preferred choice to fulfil your social needs.

From research and clinical experience, Young found that teens who struggle with anxiety, depression, stress, limited social skills and social exclusion are more likely to use SM as a psychological escape. She also points out that to break free, the starting point is to recognise the problem, admit it, and no longer be in denial.

Once the problem is recognised, it's important to take a step further and identify the core reason for this addictive behaviour. As highlighted earlier, the thing you are consuming is not the core reason for the addiction. It's what's beneath the surface.

"Addiction begins with the hope that something 'out there' can instantly fill up the emptiness inside."
— Jean Kilbourne

What is currently missing in your life where you have allowed SM overconsumption to fill in your emotional needs?
Your response will determine both the *immediate* solutions (see step 2) and *ongoing* solutions (see step 3). For example, in the analogy of weight loss, if the problem is an addiction to chocolate, then a plan is required to not only break the chocolate eating habit, but finding food alternatives to ensure long term sustainability and balance.

As highlighted in chapter three, teens are hungry to feel connected, loved and worthy, and will seek outlets if they do not get enough of this from real-life relationships. SM is just an outlet, like substances and gangs. That's why individuals who do not feel connected, loved and worthy are constantly compelled to post up the most glamorous and filtered photos for likes, comments and shares to feel connected, loved and worthy. It's a feel-good strategy. If offline relationships provided this, there wouldn't be the compulsion and urge to seek it from the online world.

The emotional starvation in the real world leads to disconnection from the real world and connection to the online world for the feelings of connection, love and worthiness to be felt.

Delving even deeper, a lack of a social life, social skills, regular face-to-face communication with family and friends, and not engaging in non technological activities furthers loneliness, and therefore, offline disconnection.

The habit of jumping online is also driven by the anxiety of not wanting to miss out on the latest updates, associated with the desire to be connected and up to date always. It's usually why the addicted jump online at every spare opportunity and perform finger exercises as they mindlessly scroll through newsfeeds, searching without purpose and wasting time.

Consider moments when you are in a face-to-face conversation with someone, studying, watching TV, or even at a concert. If you feel the urge to jump online in these moments, you may have a problem.

2) TAKE EXTREME ACTION IMMEDIATELY

Breaking free requires a *willingness* to change, a *reason* to change, and *taking extreme action immediately* to change.

A willingness to change is born when you're not prepared to accept and tolerate the harmful impact of your addiction. To find evidence of the impact, tune in and reflect. You can look back over just the past week, month or year. Unless you find evidence through reflection, then you won't have a strong reason to change. External notifications may awaken you, but it's the internal realisation and the feeling of unbearable hurt and suffering that will ignite the will to change.

Do you know how much time you spend on SM a day?
Consider this by also reflecting on the amount of time not spent on the important things in the offline world, like school work, sport, interacting with family and friends, and your own emotional well-being. Journal your thoughts and feelings, and do not hold back. Be brutally honest with yourself.

Spend a weekend without your phone and internet access. It will not only free your mind and give you space to reflect, but it will also enable you to appreciate the experience of life temporarily without technology. You will awaken to the beauty you're missing out on offline, giving you greater reasons to change.

> _When Trung hit rock bottom, he'd had enough after seeing the harmful impact of his addiction. It was killing him. He wanted out but didn't know how. The writing was on the wall. He was on a dead-end path unless he changed. The words of his loving mother gave him a reason to, and he took extreme action immediately when the opportunity arose to leave the addiction cage._

Taking extreme action immediately relates to changing your SM account settings to block opportunities for you to continue with addictive habits and behaviour. Addiction is fuelled by habit like when people unconsciously check their feeds at every spare moment without thinking.

Here are a few suggestions to break unhealthy habits and to drop your SM usage to a moderate level:

- Turn off or delete SM applications on your phone so they're not easily accessible
- Turn off auto-password on your internet browser, so each time you want to jump on, the password requirement is a cue to make you reconsider jumping online and to ensure it is purposeful
- If required, install software to temporarily block you from SM and other addictive sites. Some smartphone applications, like Moment, also track the daily usage of your phone and SM applications

Feel free to add your own. Remember, the goal is to block windows of opportunity that easily draw you online and keep you on for excessive amounts of time.

3) STICKING TO IT

Unless the root cause of SM addiction is addressed, it becomes difficult to sustain the moderate usage achieved when taking extreme action immediately, and easy to slip back into unhealthy addictive habits and behaviours.

The three main drivers of SM addiction are **not feeling connected, loved and worthy enough** offline, creating that emotional void, in which SM becomes an outlet to fill.

There are three ways to achieve a healthy relationship with SM to create lasting change and freedom from the addiction cage.

First, **seek offline alternatives to connect** with people by changing your environment. It could be through sport, church, community youth groups, hobbies and so forth. Seek positive relationships with individuals who are encouraging and supportive. Allocate time to spend on hobbies and interests that you are passionate about like fitness, art, music, writing, mediation, and helping the poor. Engage in face-to-face quality conversations with family over dinner, and with friends when you're out.

If you feel like you're struggling to find offline alternatives, then you're not trying hard enough. There are abundant opportunities. You can seek guidance and ideas from your circle of support and from Uncle Google as well. Seek, with a goal, and you will find.

Second, **schedule daily usage and limit yourself**, otherwise it's easy to lose control and get carried away. A healthy recommended daily intake is once to twice a day, for a specified duration. A maximum of one hour per day is optimal.

Third, **set connection boundaries** so you do not jump online during quality and intimate interactions with family and friends. It is time that is to be protected, appreciated and cherished. For example, when it's meant to be family time, ensure you're offline and totally devoted to family time, and not multi-tasking and only half paying attention to family members.

Feel free to add things to the list that you can do that do not involve your phone and internet access.

It's about making healthy lifestyle changes to not only create balance and sustain moderate SM usage, but to also secure feelings of connection, love and worthiness from real people in the real world.

It's at this point when you can feel truly independent. It's when you learn to set boundaries for when and how you use SM so it doesn't rob you of the best quality and greatest experience of life. That's when you can truly be free and fulfilled.

EXERCISE

Complete the following:

- Complete Dr Young's internet addiction test. If the results show that you are addicted to SM, write down how you feel when you are urged and compelled to use SM. Reflect on how it may serve you emotionally to enable you to arrive at the core root of the addictive behaviour.

- List your three most addictive SM behaviours. For each one, write down one action you can take to stop this behaviour immediately.

- To ensure the transition from addiction to moderation is long-lasting, list three offline alternatives for you to connect with others and engage in real-life activity that will serve you emotionally and disable the need or urge to jump online excessively.

SUMMARY

1. Addiction is the condition of having a *dependency/ craving/obsession* to a substance or activity that is *pleasurable*, and is *repeated*, despite the substantial harm and interference it can cause with everyday life. SM use can often lead to addiction.

2. Addiction is more than just 'chemical hooks'; it's caused by a deeper emotional void. The three main drivers of SM addiction are *not feeling connected, loved* and *worthy enough* offline, which help to create an emotional void where SM fills it.

3. Reducing SM usage to a moderate level can be achieved by taking extreme action immediately and changing SM account settings. These actions can evade windows of opportunity to connect mindlessly.

   Sustaining moderate usage over the long term can be achieved by creating healthier solutions to fill the emotional void, like seeking offline alternatives to connect, scheduling a daily usage limit, and setting connection boundaries.

8. MATES WITH FAILURE

"I have not failed. I have just found 10,000 ways that won't work."
— Thomas Edison

Jacob's life turned upside down after an ugly end to a three-year relationship with a girl. At the time, the aftermath got dangerous after Jacob received serious threats from his ex-girlfriend's new boyfriend, and led to involving the police. On advice from police, Jacob was forced to change schools for his safety and to cut all ties from his former school, which meant having to leave long-term friends and being forced to start afresh.

For the first few months at his new school in Year 11, Jacob had no friends and found it difficult to fit in and belong to a like-minded group. By term one of Year 12, his grades dropped severely, from eighties and nineties to failing several subjects. He suffered from stress and anxiety when in the exam room and found it hard to believe that there was still enough time in his final year to raise his results back up to where they were previously.

After being forced to change schools due to his relationship break-up and experiencing a significant drop in grades, Jacob's self image took a blow and he felt like a failure.

The fear of failure is natural. Nobody likes to lose, miss out or be rejected.

Failure is defined by your perspective when it shows up, which in turn determines the meaning you give it.

When referring to **becoming mates with failure**, I'm referring to developing a positive relationship with failure, so rather than fearing it or being crushed by it, you can embrace it and use it to elevate your life.

Becoming mates with failure enables you to gain valuable lessons from every experience so you can take corrective action and grow to where you want to be. You'll be strengthened from embracing failure because you're prepared to learn as you go. You will learn so much about yourself that you wouldn't have learnt otherwise.

In life, sometimes you win, sometimes you lose. Becoming mates with failure enhances your mental toughness so you can handle situations where you do lose, or when things don't go to plan. It awakens you to see the positives in every setback, because there are always positives in every setback, only to be seen when not blinded by the setback.

The ultimate recipe for success is failure. By wearing the right lenses, a setback is a setup for future success. There are no limits as to what you can achieve when you are not held back by failure. Both famous and everyday examples in history reveal that when embraced, failure forms the foundation of all great achievements.

If you do not become mates with failure, you'll be less likely to pick yourself back up and try again after getting knocked down. Lies such as 'you're not good enough' can easily make their way into your mind, damaging your self-image and igniting negative emotions. You'll be less inclined to stretch yourself and try new things, especially if they are outside of your comfort zone. Being in this state is crippling and diminishes your ability to envision the possibilities and opportunities that are still available to you whilst you are still at school, and also once you leave school.

In his first semester exams of Year 12, Jacob was sitting in a Maths exam, feeling extremely cold. His palms were sweating and he was unable to control his nerves. Deep down, he wanted to do well. Despite failing the exam, it proved to be a blessing in disguise, because it awakened him to the realisation that he only had a short amount of time to make his final year count.

It was sink or swim.

Choosing to swim, Jacob took back control when he began

feeding his mind with positive thoughts, such as 'I can get back on track', 'It's never too late', and 'I'm going to give it my all', rather than feeding it with anger, blame and excuses connected to past failures.

He returned from school holidays powered up, motivated and prepared for the tough journey ahead. To motivate himself, Jacob searched for techniques online. There was one in particular where he wrote down what he wanted to achieve and placed it where he could regularly see it. He needed a mark of 85.7 to get into the Bachelor of Construction Management and Property, so he wrote 'I will obtain a mark of 90' and placed it on his desk. This motivated him each day.

Over time, Jacob became more grateful for past events, such as taking the advice of the police on moving schools, and ending an unhealthy relationship which he learned a great deal from.

Jacob gained courage and strength through prayer and attending church every Sunday, serving his spiritual needs and beliefs that there was a higher power guiding him towards success.

Rather than allowing failure to define him and hold him back, Jacob chose to become mates with failure. Through consistent effort, motivation and perseverance, Jacob grew over time, and rose above his challenges and setbacks. He achieved a final mark of 88.1, which gained him entry into the course he wanted.

For the remaining parts of this chapter, I will share how you can become mates with failure and develop that positive relationship that is essential for your future growth, success and resilience.

In doing so, visualise failure as a real person standing in front of you, acting as a metaphor for failure. Give this person a name.

For practical purposes, let's use the name 'Francis'.

Every time Francis shows up in the form of failure, through a process of reflection, there are three *powerful* phrases to say to Francis to develop a healthy relationship and become best mates with failure.

PHRASE 1: "Hey, Francis! Thanks for showing up, mate. Look, it's okay. I'm not going to take it personally."

While completing my second year of university, studying a Bachelor of Commerce, I was keen to land some work experience as a junior trainee accountant. So I applied for thirty-five jobs over several months and was rejected every time. It was extremely disheartening.

Did I fail? Yes, at that specific point in time I did. Each rejection was a failure. Does that make me a failure? Only if I stopped and gave up. But I kept going. I didn't take the rejections personally.

After six months of consistent hunting and applying, I received a phone call while at university from a private number. It was Wayne, the owner of an accounting firm near my university.

Wayne asked if I could come in for an interview. I was so stunned that my immediate response was "NOW?", not realising what I had just said. It was a kneejerk reaction, given that his office was a ten-minute drive from university.

Wayne replied, "If you can come in now, then sure." I responded with, "But I'm not dressed appropriately." He responded, "That's okay – no need to worry about that." With a huge burst of excitement, I rushed to my car after the call, and arrived at reception within twenty minutes.

After waiting nervously to appear, Wayne and I greeted each other and within ten minutes of chatting, he offered me the position of junior accountant, my very first 'suited-up corporate role', while I was dressed in my Hawaiian shirt, shorts and sandals.

Fast forward ten plus years, I've worked with some of Australia's leading accounting firms on the back of that lucky break. I had to swallow the thirty-five rejections to get my lucky break. But was it really luck, though?

Francis appeared many times on my journey and will appear on your journey at some stage too.

There is a big difference between failing at something and feeling like a failure. Many people read the word 'failure' as FAIL-U-ARE – allowing failure to define them as a person. They are crushed by failure rather than being challenged by it.

For example, two people who fail the same exam, or do not make the team they strived for, or get rejected by the same job interviewer, can view the same experience in a totally different way. One person can be crushed by the experience, igniting negative crippling emotions. The other person can be challenged and motivated by the experience. The latter person's chances of success in that area which they failed in will increase because they did not take the experience personally and because they have a growth mindset.

It is okay to fail but do not allow failure to define you as a person. It's just an event among many events in life.

There is power in acknowledgement. Did you give that performance your best shot? Be honest with yourself when reflecting upon the reasons why you did fail because it will empower you to see failure as just a one off event, so you do not take it personally.

A lack of ability is not always the reason why people fail. Other factors may influence performance, such as circumstances outside of their control affecting preparation (e.g. family problems, personal issues).

Don't be too harsh on yourself. Show self-compassion and treat failings as isolated experiences, and not a reflection of your potential. Tomorrow is always a brand new day.

When feeling like a failure, self-compassion expert Dr. Kristin Neff encourages individuals to consider how they would feel if they started treating themselves like they would treat a friend.

According to Dr Neff, writing a letter to yourself from the perspective of a good friend and reading it out loud will strengthen you to accept your failings, and ignite kindness and self-love to help you move forward and accept everything about yourself that makes up your S.T.U.F.F.

Real failure is when you don't try at all.

PHRASE 2: "Thanks, mate! I've learned so much having gone through this."

When starting out as a professional Master of Ceremonies (MC), I was given the opportunity to host my first wedding. It was a small affair, only eighty people. Culturally, the bride and groom were Anglo-Australian. It was also my first paid role. My dream was becoming a reality.

With little experience, the night unfolded into my worst nightmare. Midway through, Giuseppe, the reception owner, took me outside and provided some 'nice' feedback using colourful language. He was a very passionate Italian man, who I knew only had the customers' best interests in mind when giving the feedback.

Harsh words were said and I felt so gutted. I tried not to take it personally but it was difficult in the heat of the moment. Once the wedding was over, I returned home at 1 am and wept. I felt like my dream had been crushed before my eyes. But the passion, fire and burning desire running through me was not going to allow that experience to be the end of the journey.

Unable to sleep, I grabbed a pen and paper and wrote down all the feedback that Giuseppe provided. He shared wisdom that was to my advantage, not detriment, and I wanted to keep a record for future reference. I needed to take on board the comments as constructive feedback in order to move forward. After writing everything down, my pain, frustration and hurt turned into motivation. My motto became 'I will until'.

I still have Giuseppe's comments to this day which I refer to from time to time. Looking back, I am forever grateful for failing miserably early on, and even more grateful for the pearls of wisdom that I received from Giuseppe. They became my foundational building blocks to grow into one of Australia's leading MCs, turning my dream into reality.

Every failure is a valuable experience – only if you have an open mind to learn in spite of painful experiences - otherwise you'll walk away empty from each experience.

Each experience can either act as a building block or stumbling block towards success. It's your response to each experience that will determine which it will be.

You can ensure every experience is a building block by:

- taking responsibility for where you're at and not blaming others
- taking initiative by asking questions and seeking constructive feedback

- documenting constructive feedback so you can always refer to it to guide you forward
- internalising gratitude for the teachings and lessons that each experience provides

You fail when you do not learn anything – in both failure and success.

PHRASE 3: "Okay, mate! It's time for me to move on. Thanks for the fuel."

In the first term of Year 12, my grades were just scraping a pass.

At times during that year, I became disheartened when receiving assessment marks less than expected, especially after pouring everything I had into them.

On one occasion, I handed in a business studies assignment without my name on it. Once the marked assignments were being handed out to students, I saw a mark of twenty out of twenty on my copy. I was over the moon. Once the teacher found out that it was my assignment, it was redirected to the subject coordinator for remarking, and I was given a 'revised' final mark of sixteen out of twenty, without knowing why. I was really disappointed, not by the result, but by the subject coordinator's perception of me. He didn't believe it was my work given my poor academic track record. My self-image took a blow.

Despite being gutted, I was not going to allow myself to be derailed by it. I chose to use the downgrade as fuel to prove to the subject coordinator that I was capable of producing high-quality work. By the end of Year 12, I was listed in the top 10% of Australia for that subject.

With the right perspective and willingness to learn, failure can become a source of unexpected motivation, providing the fuel you need to move forward from your experiences and on your way to success – but only if you allow it to.

By persisting to continually improve, success becomes only a matter of time. A person only becomes a failure once they believe they are, once they stop trying and once they give up.

Failure is not a lifetime sentence. It's an event, and it's important to see beyond that event into a future with endless possibilities and opportunities. You just have to stay in the game.

"Failure will never overtake me if my determination to succeed is strong enough."
– Og Mandino

In an interview, Arnold Schwarzenegger once shared how he cried all night after losing a competition when he was only twenty-one years old, having arrived newly to America with the dream of becoming a world bodybuilding champion.

When he eventually picked himself back up, Arnold kept thinking about the reason why he was in America in the first place - to beat all the American bodybuilders and all the bodybuilders around the world. Despite the setbacks, Arnold turned his dream into reality, winning the Mr Olympia contest seven times.

Just like Arnold, when you do fall down, be reminded of your driving force. Be careful not to judge too early and predict prematurely what's possible for you based on an experience. Change and growth isn't overnight. Allow yourself time to apply the lessons gained from your failures into future experiences, and only evaluate yourself after applying these lessons. You will see the value of these lessons reflected in the progress and improvement that you make, which is motivating and confidence-building.

By not applying what you learn into future experiences, it's as Ted Nicholas once said: "Knowledge without action is like having no knowledge at all."

As you're reading this chapter, you may be asking yourself, 'What if I do not get the results I need in my final Year 12 exams to get into the course I want?'

Consider Shammah's story.

After being the first student in school history to repeat Year 11, Shammah went on to fail Year 12 miserably. She was one of four students out of a cohort of one-hundred-and-fifty students that didn't graduate with a final number because it was so low.

Not knowing what to do with her life, Shammah took the advice and recommendation of a family friend to take up a course in business marketing at a private business college.

Starting a new page in an area which she loved, Shammah began to shine, topping her class. Fearless and driven, she did something that had never been done previously. A process that would normally be filled with bureaucracy and red tape, Shammah approached her teacher at college with a proposal to present to the Board of Education to allow her to progress directly into the second year of university, provided that she was able to maintain a distinction average. The proposal was presented and the board approved.

Despite failing the 'all important' final year of school miserably, Shammah did not allow it to define her and to block her from moving forward to create her own path.

After completing her studies and becoming a successful business advisor for entrepreneurs, Shammah went on to create her own path once again by becoming a wellness coach and committing her life to supporting the wellbeing of others. Through the journey of overcoming failure, adversity and setbacks, Shammah discovered her true purpose in life.

It's not the end of the world if you don't do as well as you hoped in your exams. The reality is that not everyone does well in a school environment.

When you want something bad enough in spite of failure, possibilities emerge when you dream up pathways and find a trusted adult who can mentor and guide you.

Sometimes, success doesn't come right away. It may take longer than expected, and it might come in different ways to what was previously hoped for.

No matter which path you take, a positive attitude, hunger and outlook will always ensure you'll gain valuable experience from your pursuit.

You never know what other opportunities are hidden along the way that will change your life direction, and that will reveal the beautiful serendipities of life.

EXERCISE

Complete the following:

- Reflect upon one recent experience of failure (e.g. exam result, loss in sport, poor on-stage performance, relationship breakup, unsuccessful job interview). Describe your feelings, self-talk, and perspective i) at the time of the experience, and ii) several weeks later.

From reflecting upon this experience, does it reveal that a) you embraced failure and gained great benefits from it, or that b) you were shattered by it, which damaged your self-image?

- Write down one phrase of your own that you can affirm in future experiences to develop a positive relationship with failure. This will enhance your positive perspective towards it, enable you to progress from it, and empower you to persevere through it.

- Using Dr Neff's advice in relation to exercising self-compassion, write a short letter to yourself from the perspective of a good friend. For future reference, have one on file to read out aloud in the aftermath of a failure to strengthen you to move forward and ignite self-love.

SUMMARY

1. The fear of failure is natural. Your perspective when you do fail determines the meaning you give it. Develop a positive relationship with failure, so rather than fearing it or being crushed by it, you can embrace it and use it to elevate your life.

2. Every failure can either act as a building block or stumbling block towards success. It's your response to each experience that will determine which it will be. A person only becomes a failure once they believe they are, once they stop trying and once they give up.

3. To develop a positive relationship with failure, visualise Francis every time you fail. Let Francis know three things about the experience: that you're not going to take the failure personally, that you've learned so much from it, and that you're thankful for the fuel it has provided you to move on and persevere.

9. BEAT THE BULLY

"No one can make you feel inferior without your consent."
— Eleanor Roosevelt

*L*ouise was fourteen when a photo was taken up her dress by a girl and shared digitally to the entire school.

While Louise struggled to fit in growing up, the photo became the catalyst for her becoming a constant target for nasty verbal insults, especially in relation to her physical appearance. In class, she would be laughed at and ridiculed by everyone for her 'elephant thighs' and 'how a whale can survive out of water.'

Over time, bullies began physically attacking Louise. When walking into the school bathroom, she would be surrounded and pushed around by a group of girls. When walking home from school, she would often be hit in the back by passing bullies.

For someone who only had love to share, it was a very difficult time for Louise, as she found herself in the bully target zone.

As highlighted earlier, your teen years are a journey of discovering who you are, the person you'd like to be, and, while you're at it, figuring out where and how you can fit in socially so others can like and accept you.

The reality is, no matter at what age, some people will like you and others won't. You'll gain friends, you'll lose friends, and just like Louise, myself and many teens today, you may find yourself in the bully target zone because you're seen as different in some way.

The 'Bullying No Way' website defines bullying as the ongoing misuse of power in relationships through repeated verbal, physical and/or social behaviour that causes physical and/or psychological harm.

Bullies are not fussy when it comes to looking for individuals they can overpower and dominate. They'll find a reason to pick on anyone – tall kids, short kids, smart kids, nerds, black kids, white kids, different interests, the way you walk or talk, etc – and deliberately find weaknesses they can exploit. They'll do whatever it takes to overpower you, like using offensive language and physical violence, manipulating and using you, and posting embarrassing and cruel comments or photos online.

Whether you're bullied online or offline, you still retain the freedom to choose either to allow bullies to dictate your feelings, choices and experiences or to take control of your own security and happiness by building your mental and emotional resilience. The latter will give you what I call **the mental edge** over your bullies.

With the mental edge, you'll become thick-skinned and feel safe in your own skin. You'll develop greater emotional intelligence and social skills to effectively deal with verbal and virtual bullying and not allow the immaturity and insecurities of others to rob you of joy.

You'll be empowered to embrace your uniqueness and the truth of who you really are, and not what others label you to be, which will increase your self-confidence.

Rather than being distracted by bullies standing in the way of your success and happiness, the mental edge will enable you to focus on the important things in life, like school, family, your future, allowing you to fearlessly pursue the path that your heart desires to achieve your dreams.

When growing up, I loved listening to music and had a collection of soundtracks of my favourite artists. My favourite songs were always on repeat and I knew all the lyrics off by heart. Hearing those songs today would take me back and resurrect the feelings and emotions I had during that time and allow me to reminisce and relive those experiences through my memory. Those songs became part of my internal fabric.

In life, you have the freedom to choose the soundtrack that plays over and over again on your journey – the soundtrack of truth or the soundtrack of lies. Whichever you choose, it will become part of your internal fabric.

The soundtrack of truth will give you the mental edge when deliberately played by choice, not chance.

By not pressing play on the soundtrack of truth, the soundtrack of lies plays by default, initially heard through a soft volume, and then gradually intensifies when you allow the words and gestures of bullies to easily define you.

These experiences become the lyrics and music that create negative thought patterns, and if played over and over again for long enough, these lyrics will be learned off by heart, shaping negative beliefs that make you feel powerless.

You start believing things like you are not good enough, that you are not loved, and you cannot do anything great in your life – simply because you have allowed yourself to listen to the wrong soundtrack.

For a boxer to beat opponents in the boxing ring, physical strength, while needed, is not as important as mental strength when it comes to persevering for twelve or more rounds of fighting.

Every day when you wake up, you are stepping into the 'ring of life' – where you may face bullies. It could be when you catch the bus to school, in the playground, in the classroom, and even virtually on social media.

With headphones on and listening to her favourite song on the bus ride home, Louise received a sudden punch to the back of the head by another girl. Feeling furious and her blood boiling, she turned around with her fist raised, ready to inflict the same pain, but froze while her fist was midway in the air, inches away from the girl's face.

In that one split second, it was like Louise's entire life came to a standstill and flashing before her eyes were her dreams, goals and aspirations, awakening her to the fear that if her fist connected, she would get suspended, crushing her deepest desires for the future. The pain of not becoming a prefect and joining the student representative council at her school was greater than the pain of the punch she received to the back of the head.

Rather than fighting back with her fist, Louise turned around in her seat and just laughed, knowing that she had just chosen her future over revenge. While the bully thought they succeeded in physically hurting her, Louise knew in her mind that she was stronger and her response showed that.

Following the bus incident, Louise dealt with bullies by drawing strength from her innate qualities of empathy, compassion and love, which enabled her to see the hurtful behaviour of bullies as a reflection of the hurt they have within themselves.

Louise chose to practise forgiveness by treating bullies like she wanted to be treated. Bullies were confused by how she responded, and her response made it much more difficult for them to continue hassling her.

Louise stayed true to herself and to what she stood for, embracing the truth of her identity, worth and potential to do great things with her gifts. She embraced the things she enjoyed, like studying, learning, laughing, and, most of all, being a role model for other people.

She knew that if she wasn't able to control her state of mind, she wouldn't be able to help others, so she deliberately immersed herself in positive resources online via YouTube that helped her control her emotional state and retain focus on the right things.

Her mantra was that everything gets better in the end, and if it's not better, it's not the end.

Over time, Louise's peers saw the beautiful qualities that she chose to display and what she stood for: unity, respect, kindness, playfulness and intelligence. She went from being in the bully target zone to becoming the most popular person at school – for the right reasons – and gaining the respect of those who once bullied her.

By developing the mental edge, Louise beat the bullies without throwing a single punch.

For the remaining parts of this chapter, I will share how, by developing the mental edge, you can beat the bully in the ring of life without throwing a single punch – just like Louise.

In doing so, I will be drawing on the similarities between the mental edge strategies that a boxer applies to defeat opponents in the boxing ring, and the mental edge strategies that you can apply to beat the bully in the ring of life, without needing to throw a single punch.

BE TOUGH

Before stepping into the ring, the boxer knows that it's more than just a battle of physical strength, skill and speed with their opponent. It's a mental fight – a battle between two minds – and victory will go to the one with the mental edge.

In training and preparation, the boxer not only builds physical strength and stamina through weightlifting and cardio aerobic exercise, but also their mental strength by learning strategies and techniques so they can fearlessly step into the ring and respond with confidence when punches are thrown at them. Without mental strength, every punch thrown will connect and hurt, giving the boxer little chance to become victorious.

I endured many things from name-calling, social exclusion and racial attacks to being pushed around and punched at almost every day. Even when I joined the weekend rugby league team, I became a bully target for my own teammates, who ganged up on me and always put me down at training sessions. I thought it was just part of growing up.

Throughout primary school and the early stages of high school, I didn't handle bullies well. When trying to defend myself, I'd throw mean, nasty and derogatory words back at bullies, only to add fuel to the fire. I was too young to understand that two wrongs do not make a right. The more angry and upset I got, the more bullies would continue giving me a hard time.

I never used violence to retaliate, but only in self-defence. That changed on the eve of my Year 6 graduation ceremony. After constantly being hassled by Kevin over a period of time, I exploded one recess while on the basketball court and gave him a black eye. The result? Kevin never hassled me again and I carried a macho mentality into high school.

In Year 8, I discovered the power of the boomerang effect after an incident with Trent. A new student on a rugby league scholarship, Trent was big, strong and extremely talented. We first met at a training session. I was in the second division team and he was in the first division. Over several months, Trent continuously picked on me with insulting comments, and tried to intimidate me with his size. But I kept my cool, until one morning during our Design and Technology class, things got heated after Trent started racially abusing me. I snapped and physically retaliated, but I ended up with a black eye, concussed and suspended from school.

Trent taught me a valuable lesson: that if violence was to be used against bullies to 'teach a lesson', then it's only a matter of time before being on the receiving end of someone who is physically stronger, which in some cases can lead to fatal consequences. After that, the macho mentality got trashed, and I decided to not respond to bullies with violence again.

I wasn't left with many strategies other than to become mentally tough enough to suck it up and to build my resilience. If I could just be totally ignorant and avoid responding with anger, it's only a matter of time before bullies would get sick of speaking to a brick wall.

I took responsibility for what was in my control, like how I responded to bullies, and acknowledging the things that weren't, like how bullies behaved.

When I started training at the gym at fourteen, it built my physical strength, appearance and self-confidence, making it harder for bullies to rattle me, not because I was physically bigger or stronger, but because I felt stronger internally.

I became more deliberate about staying clear of the path of bullies to avoid being in the target zone for attack. Whenever bullies verbally attacked, I ignored them, laughed it off or just walked away. I stopped caring. I refrained from retaliating to avoid giving them the satisfaction of luring me into a fight. I'd been there, done that many times, to no avail.

In what appeared to be a softer approach to dealing with bullies, it made me stronger mentally and emotionally. That's when I became really tough and thick-skinned. By making it so hard for bullies to upset me with their words, they gave up over time.

In the ring of life, you become confident, fearless and mentally tough when you learn how to respond when bullies throw punches in the form of mean and nasty words. Bullies want the mental edge over you and you give that to them when you allow them to easily upset you. Whilst you cannot control when bullies strike, you are in 100% control of the effect their words have on you. You need to be tough, thick-skinned and not easily rattled.

Rather than resorting to verbal and physical attacks, there are three ways to fearlessly and confidently respond to bullies so they can be silenced and left powerless.

The first is **using non-confrontational language.**

Famous actress Salma Hayek's approach to responding to bullies when they pick up on weaknesses is with two words: "So what."

For example, if a bully picks on you for the way you look, speak, walk, or even a mistake you made, just respond with non-confrontational language like "So what" and "Thanks for the heads-up." It silences them and is a great way to disable, diffuse and disarm the power that bullies are trying to inflict. If you retaliate, they will keep going. Don't try and win the war of words, because it will just make things worse.

When bullies see that you're unaffected by their words, they'll more than likely find someone else to target and upset to give them that 'feel good' feeling since they couldn't get it from hassling you.

With a smile, the second is to **always agree** with bullies, even if their comments make you furious on the inside. This is what being tough is all about – the ability to control your emotions, especially anger, and to not give power to the words that bullies throw at you.

While you may think this is ridiculous, it actually works. Your response would totally surprise them. It's not what they're wanting and expecting. They want to upset and hurt you. You do not give them that satisfaction when you agree with them. When you agree with them, they'll end up running out of things to say because you've remained thick-skinned. Eventually, they'll give up and shut up. The alternative is to disagree, and to start a war of words that will only make you angrier, and your bullies happier. Ignorance is bliss.

For example, if a bully says, "You're weird", "You're annoying", "You're fat" or "Nobody likes you," you can, with a smile, respond with something like, "You know what, you've got a point. We all can't be as lucky as you," and just walk away.

In fact, responding like this will make your bully look like an idiot because you're unaffected by their comments. Deep down, you know who you are, and that's all that matters.

The third is **treating others like you want to be treated**.

"Am I not destroying my enemies when I make friends of them?"
— Abraham Lincoln

It's easier said than done, right? But that's what it takes to build strength and be mentally tough. When you are always nice to someone who is giving you a hard time, it's very difficult for them to have the heart to keep giving you a hard time. Bullies are people who are usually hurting the most, and are thirsty for love. Practising empathy, compassion and forgiveness towards bullies strengthens your acceptance for who you are, and silences them.

A person does not wake up one day and decide, 'Hey, I'm going to become a bully.' Quite often, bullies are unaware that their behaviour is bullying.

So what causes someone to become a bully?

Common reasons include personal issues, being or looking 'cool', emotional neglect, jealousy, peer group protection or even being victims of bullying themselves. Research even shows that individuals who are bullies at school find themselves with mental health issues later in life and are likely to engage in criminal and antisocial behaviour.

Don't be fooled: the problem lies with the bully, not you. Their behaviour is a reflection of themselves. Bullies are not liked by the majority, even though they may give the impression they are strong and popular.

While many bullies are non-violent and just immature, you need to be weary of bullies who are more likely to use violence. They will try and catch you off guard by firmly pushing you from behind, grabbing your wrists or putting you in a headlock. Taking up martial arts and defensive training will make you feel confident that you can defend yourself.

Where possible, avoid being lured into a fight, as they carry serious risks to your safety, but when required, be prepared to defend and protect yourself from harm, and seek adult intervention.

EMBRACE THE TRUTH

Every time before stepping into the ring and throwing the first punch, the boxer must conquer their doubt and insecurities to believe they are *good* enough, *strong* enough and *skilled* enough to beat their opponent. Without such confidence and conviction in themselves, their opponent will walk all over them once they're in battle.

"If there is no enemy within – the enemy outside can do us no harm."
— African Proverb

Beating the bully around you starts by beating the bully within you – that is, your negative self-talk, shared through the story of the two wolves in chapter three.

Every time before stepping into the ring of life and even before the first word is said to you, you feel confident, fearless and strong when you know your S.T.U.F.F, your worth and your potential. This is the fullness of your truth (as discussed in chapters two, three and four) and believing this truth will allow you to feel safe in your own skin.

Everyone is different and unique. When you love yourself and accept your uniqueness, it's very difficult to be rattled by the words that bullies say.

In an interview with Ellen DeGeneres, superstar Justin Timberlake shared how he was verbally and physically bullied because he was different. He said, "I grew up in Tennessee, and if you didn't play football, you were a sissy. I got slurs all the time because I was in music and art... I was an outcast in a lot of ways... but everything that you get picked on for or you feel makes you weird is essentially what's going to make you sexy as an adult."

Justin not only survived teen bullying because he embraced the fullness of his truth, but also thrived as an adult because of that truth. The very reason that he was bullied turned out to be the thing that allowed him to become successful in adulthood. Justin maintained the mental edge and beat the bullies.

Bullies don't like to see people who shine and stand out, and are different. It exposes their insecurities and makes them want to inflict hurt on others.

AWAKEN YOUR DRIVE

The boxer steps into the ring not because they are bored, lonely and trying to fill up spare time. They are pulled towards something that is meaningful to them like the desire to be a winner, their passion towards the sport, and the drive to achieve sporting mastery. These reasons become the fuel and motivation that builds the mental strength needed to not only fearlessly step in the ring, but also to persevere especially during the most difficult rounds.

When American singer Taylor Swift was bullied during high school, she used her experiences as a driving force for her passion: music. When she was twelve, she started writing songs about her experiences, such as not being invited to a birthday party, not feeling included, wishing she had more friends, and about constantly being picked on.

Rather than being held back by believing the lies around her, instead she believed in herself, the truth of her worth, and directed her energy and emotions into her musical passion. Awakening her drive empowered Taylor to move past her bullying experiences, and turning that drive into a successful career in music.

This is one of countless, global stories when teens channelled their drive and turned their painful bullying experiences into motivation towards their passions, goals and aspirations. In moving forward, they drew inspiration from the things in their life that gave them most joy and happiness.

Personal joy and happiness is an inside job created by you. Don't leave it in another person's control.

Here are a few ideas to draw inspiration from:

- Faith
- Family and friends, companionship
- Dreams
- Music, writing, art
- Inspirational people
- Recognition and respect
- Proving people wrong

Internalising these positive drivers, rather than negative emotions, will not only make you stronger and resilient, but also will give your life hope, meaning and vision.

TURN TO SUPPORT

After each round, the boxer heads to the corner of the ring to catch their breath, rehydrate, and be treated for injuries. Most importantly, however, is that they take comfort and are lifted by words of encouragement from their coach so they can persevere.

Sometimes, bullies are really persistent, and don't give up even after you've exhausted the above strategies shared.

"Ask for help. Not because you are weak. But because you want to remain strong."
— Les Brown

It takes courage and bravery to break through your fears and reach out for support.

You may fear being labelled a dobber and making thing worse. You may fear being let down and not receiving the support you need. You won't know until you try, and until you do, it's not true.

Reach out to your circle of support, including the leaders and anti-bullying ambassadors at your school. Most school websites have an online form that can be completed to report bullying. Identify the person at your school whom you feel most comfortable speaking with, and make time to see them and talk about what you are going through, as well as to seek guidance in how to deal with it.

Most students do not support bullying if you asked them, so be confident that you will be supported.

Change your perspective about speaking up – from worrying about being seen as a dobber to someone who initiates a positive change. To be empowered, ask yourself if the opinions of others matter in five years' time.

It's hard to believe that speaking up is a blessing in disguise for the bullies, but it actually creates a starting point to solve the problems that they are experiencing. You are helping the bully as much as you are by standing up for yourself.

Speaking up indirectly helps others who are also being bullied, in many cases by the same bullies who are targeting you. Your decision to stand tall can ignite courage and inspire others to do the same, creating positive ripples of cultural change within the school to create a bully-free environment for all.

If you are a bystander and do nothing, you are supporting the actions of the bully. It takes courage to stand up and tell the bullies that their words and actions are not appropriate.

If your brother, sister, cousin or friend were being harassed, would you stand and watch?

RESPECT

From eating sardines for dinner to using candles at night for light, growing up in poverty in South Africa wasn't easy for Dr Habib Noorbhai. His parents could only afford the bare essentials at home, and at most times they struggled to put food on the table. He'd travel to school either by foot, bus or catch lifts with friends.

When Habib was eleven, his parents separated, and this proved to be an emotionally difficult time for him as he grew up loving and appreciating both parents.

Habib went to school in Johannesburg, which has one of the highest crime rates globally, and at one point or another, he was carjacked, mugged and beaten up during this time. He also witnessed several friends die right before his eyes.

Habib was a quiet person, and was reserved in social circles. When trying to blend in with others, he found it difficult and would be regularly picked on, teased and ridiculed. It didn't help that he had an unpopular, bully-friendly name.

Bullies made the extra effort to deliberately find a weakness within him to publicly insult him.

However, during high school, Habib would not retaliate with verbal and physical attacks in response to bullies. Instead, he chose to suck it up, toughen up and not allow the words of others upset him.

In Habib's mind, most of the bullies were childish, immature and had low emotional intelligence, so it was only a matter of time before they matured and grew out of their behaviour towards him. Instead, he directed his energy towards his studies, dreams and aspirations, undeterred by the background noise of bullies.

By embracing the fullness of truth in who he was and sustaining the mental edge throughout high school, Habib beat the bullies – without throwing a single punch – to create a life of achievements as a lecturer, researcher, sports scientist, speaker, author, humanitarian, and, later on, being crowned as Mr South Africa in 2017.

When in school, it's hard to believe that your bullies could one day be your friends. Several years after school, Habib crossed paths with his bullies and faced them head on, overcoming his fears to treat them with diplomacy and tact. He gained their respect.

Having matured over time, those who once bullied Habib chose to become good friends with him. They chat regularly on Facebook and are now also inspired by Habib's daily actions and look up to him as a role model. You can follow Habib's journey at habibnoorbhai.com and @Habib_Noorbhai.

Just like a professional boxing match only lasts for twelve rounds, bullying does not last forever. By building your strength, embracing your truth, awakening your drive and turning to support, you'll not only survive your bullying experiences, but also thrive because of them.

Like many success stories, you'll be thankful because these experiences made you stronger and created the opportunity for you to one day gain the respect of those who once bullied you. At that point, you can share your story of how you beat the bully, without throwing a single punch.

EXERCISE

Complete the following:

- While reading through the section on how to respond to bullies by using *non-confrontational language,* reflect upon your bullying experiences to date. Write down three non-confrontational phrases of your own that you can use to silence bullies and leave them powerless and run them past a trusted person to be safe.

Once you've received the okay, prepare yourself mentally and emotionally by visualising yourself using these phrases in the future. Practise them with confidence.

- Write down a list of positive truths about yourself, with consideration to your identity, worth and potential. (I would suggest doing this with a trusted person.) Refer to this list to empower you with the soundtrack of truth whenever bullies try and tell you otherwise to maintain the mental edge.

- Write down three trusted people whom you can turn to for support. For each trusted person, visualise i) how you would explain your experiences, and ii) the support you would like to receive from them.

SUMMARY

1. Whether you're bullied offline or online, you have the freedom to choose to either allow bullies to dictate your feelings, choices, and experiences or choose to develop 'the mental edge' over your bullies.

2. To B.E.A.T the bully without throwing a single punch, remember: Be tough, Embrace the truth, Awaken the drive and Turn to support.

3. There are three ways to silence verbal bullies and leave them powerless: use non-confrontational language, always agree with them, and treat them how you want to be treated.

---

10. UNSTOPPABLE

"Challenges are what make life interesting and overcoming them is what makes life meaningful."
— Joshua J Marine

*G*abbie was shattered midway through Year 11 when she received the news that her grandmother had passed away. As Gabbie was very close to her, she struggled dealing with her loss, getting angry quickly out of grief.

A month later, Gabbie enrolled in the Sydney City to Surf, a popular road running event covering fourteen kilometres, to raise funds for a trip to Cambodia. At the same time, she used running as an outlet to redirect her emotional energy from grief to joy. While running, Gabbie felt a twinge at the bottom of her left foot. Once passing the finish line, she was in extreme pain and became concerned.

Within days, Gabbie saw her doctor and underwent tests on her foot. On completion, her doctor advised her to undergo a foot operation on the last day of Year 11. Several days after the operation while on her break, Gabbie was shocked to receive the news that she'd been diagnosed with a rare muscle cancer called Alveolar Rhabdomyosarcoma, which has a 20% survival rate. In that one heart-stopping moment, her whole world changed completely.

After the initial shock, reality didn't start sinking in for Gabbie until chemotherapy commenced only five days after her seventeenth birthday. By that point, she had started Year 12.

Feeling overwhelmed and not in control, Gabbie struggled mentally due to many fears. She was afraid of the unknown, losing her hair, being labelled as the 'cancer girl', being treated differently, not being seen for who she is, not being able to juggle her studies and treatment, missing out on fun, not being able to cope, and not being able to make it through her final year of school.

Within just two months, Gabbie's world was hit hard by adversity and she felt life was going from bad to worse.

Like Gabbie, there will be times when life will hit you hard with unpredictable circumstances that are out of your control, like death, illness, family breakdown, injury, financial distress or any other situation outside of your direct control.

What do you do?

> From about the age of fifteen, an increasing amount of teens take up a gym membership to improve their strength, body image and overall health. The most common exercises amongst males and females are weight lifting, aerobics and cardiovascular workouts.
>
> Life is like a gym, where every day, there are opportunities to lift weights and build the most important muscle of all: **the emotional muscle.** In the gym of life, weights refer to challenges, obstacles and adversity.

Building your emotional muscle will strengthen you to cope with adversity when it strikes. You'll be empowered to take control, and to respond in a positive way that will allow you to move forward and get through your commitments.

Whilst you may not be in 100% control of how and when adversity strikes, you are in 100% control of how you respond to it. You'll develop that fighting spirit to persevere beyond what you thought was possible, building your resilience and character. You'll be able to gain a different perspective on life that will enable you to see the positive in every situation, whether good or bad.

You will also become more empathetic to others who are experiencing what you've experienced and become a source of support, hope and inspiration to them.

Life is a rollercoaster that has its ups and downs. Building your emotional muscle when you're down is a decision that only you can make. Not making a decision to build your muscle is still a decision, but with dire consequences.

> If you place both an egg and the potato in boiling water, they both come out differently once boiled. The egg will be hardened, while the potato will be softened. The boiling water represents tough times. Your decision to build will strengthen you, and your non-decision will weaken you.

If you do not build your emotional muscle, you'll become vulnerable to the three biggest enemies of success and joy: the blame game, the trap of excuses and the victim mindset.

Rather than building strength, a cycle of negative thoughts builds up stress and anxiety within and also feeds negative behaviour. You'll become emotionally crippled and unable to cope with difficult situations, and that consequence will have a negative impact on not only yourself but also your loved ones.

When teens allow themselves to be soft potatoes, rather than hard eggs, during tough times, they allow their grades to fall, they make irresponsible choices, they become associated with the wrong people, and resort to other negative avenues to support their emotional needs.

"Life is a very mean and nasty place and I don't care how tough you are, it will beat you to your knees and keep you there permanently if you let it. You, me, or nobody is going to hit as hard as life, but it ain't about how hard you hit, it's about how hard you can get hit and keep moving forward. That's how winning is done."
— Rocky Balboa,
Rocky Balboa

For the remaining parts of this chapter, I will share how you can build your emotional muscle in the gym of life so you can cope when adversity strikes and rise above your challenges.

In explaining the gym analogy, I will unpack the ingredients required to build physical muscle in the traditional gym, which are the same ingredients required to build the emotional muscle in the gym of life.

For building physical muscle in the traditional gym, I will use the example of a weightlifting bodybuilder. While this example is male-specific, female readers can apply the principles shared to other forms of exercise such as cardio and aerobics that build physical muscle.

For building emotional muscle in the gym of life, I will be drawing on Gabbie's story in how she built her emotional muscle to fight cancer, whilst completing the most important year of her life to date –Year 12.

WINNING EMOTIONS

Before every workout, a bodybuilder must be deliberate about controlling their emotions to feel empowered and strengthened to achieve their weightlifting workout goals. Taking control could be through listening to motivating music, warming up effectively, reading an inspirational message from a loved one or on the internet, or visualising their future dreams and goals.

Any one of these methods ignites positive emotions and drives out negative emotions, strengthening their emotional muscle that feeds into the strength they have to lift the weights to build their physical muscle.

Just like the bodybuilder, there'll be weight that you will be required to lift when adversity strikes in the gym of life.

There are *three stages* to dealing with adversity. The transition through all three stages reveals a person's ability to recover effectively and build resilience.

The first stage is **finding out**. The natural immediate reaction is shock and disbelief. Emotions are high, and, depending on the type of adversity, consist of a variety of the following: fear, worry, sadness, grief, anger, frustration, disappointment, blame and resentment.

The second stage is **processing** it. After the initial shock and disbelief, there is a period of time where you begin to gradually acknowledge what's happened, while still coming to terms with it. This is the most difficult period. During this period, it is still normal for negative emotions, such as sadness, to be at play. It's okay to not be okay during these times.

Society says it's not cool to cry or you're not tough if you cry. That is far from the truth. Shedding tears is not a sign of weakness. It is a sign of being human and an expression of emotion, so let it out. It's okay to cry.

Positive and negative emotions cannot occupy the mind at the same time.
Napoleon Hill

The last stage is **taking control** of your emotions. By choosing to accept what has happened, especially since it's outside of your control, you can move forward with positive emotions. By not taking control and holding onto negative emotions long enough increases the risks of mental health problems.

Once chemotherapy commenced, Gabbie was challenged physically, mentally and emotionally. She struggled to maintain focus on her studies for the most part of term one of Year 12, and also struggled with mentally preparing herself for how others would treat her once they knew she had cancer.

Early on, Gabbie often felt frustrated and discouraged, because she was missing out on the fun stuff at school like hanging out with friends, attending school shows and carnivals, and just the feeling of enjoying the last year of school. Gabbie had a heavy weight to lift, and at times she felt like there was no point of even trying.

Fear, frustration, worry and insecurity dominated Gabbie's emotional state, and she felt powerless during the initial stages of the cancer diagnosis. While the initial diagnosis and undergoing treatment were extremely difficult, Gabbie was most affected when losing her hair, because that's when the world 'knew'. At the same time, it was also a major turning point for her.

She was so surprised when others would say, "You look so much better than I thought you'd look," because leading up to her hair loss, the fear and anxiety that she'd built up mentally painted a misleading picture of how others would see and treat her.

From that point on, Gabbie decided to not allow negative emotions take a hold of her emotional state.

Determined to make her diagnosis just another obstacle, Gabbie chose to be grateful for the things she did have in her life, like a loving and supportive family, whom she always hanged out and laughed with. It allowed her to see her world through a different set of lenses and put perspective back into her life.

Gabbie realised that even though she was enduring a battle that she wouldn't wish on her worst enemy, she wasn't doing too bad, and things could be worse. She would constantly remind herself that there was always another person somewhere experiencing a tougher journey and that there was no reason why she couldn't take the cards she'd been dealt with and overcome her obstacles.

To ensure others didn't feel like they needed to treat her any different, Gabbie would deliberately make jokes about hair and start conversations about subjects unrelated to her condition, just to make things less awkward for others, and so that they had something more than just cancer to remember her by.

These positive emotions strengthened Gabbie, ignited her fighting spirit, and empowered her to accept her struggle, take control and move forward.

Being positive is a choice, and there are several ways to ignite positivity in your life.

Barbara Fredrickson, American psychologist and author of *Positivity*, explains ten most common positive emotions where research has found to shape people's lives and their potential to win: *joy, gratitude, serenity, interest, hope, pride, amusement, inspiration, awe* and *love*. These are the winning emotions.

During tough times, the most powerful winning emotion is gratitude.

Anthony Robbins says that the best thing to do when you're experiencing a difficult period is to trade what upsets you, being your expectations that are not being met, for appreciation of what you do have, and also for the things that have happened in your life – both good and bad.

By choosing to be grateful, it reminds you that no matter how bad your life appears to be, there is someone else out there fighting to survive – whether academically, socially, financially, physically or emotionally. Your entire emotional state can change in a heartbeat when you ignite feelings of gratitude.

At the end of each day, I would encourage you to:

- count the blessings in your life (e.g. your family, your house, food to eat, friends, health, physical abilities, faith, opportunities, education, past experiences and memories, the country you live in, the good times, the little things)
- identify three moments from the day that just passed that you can be grateful for (e.g. a conversation with a friend, lesson learned in a difficult situation, a joyful experience on a school excursion).

You can even create your own daily gratitude ritual that works for you.

Life is tough, but always remind yourself that it could be worse.

PROTECTION

When lifting extremely heavy weights, a bodybuilder will have a buddy who looks over each movement, not only for safety and protection but also for additional support and motivation to push beyond their limits. Without a buddy, the amount lifted wouldn't be as high as with a buddy. Even worse, the bodybuilder trying to lift very heavy weights without a buddy would lead to one thing – the weight being dropped straight onto them, causing severe damage.

Whilst everyone responds to adversity differently, research shows that the speed and ability in which individuals bounce back from adversity is highly dependent on the positive influences in their life, and their strength to seek support when needed.

Many teens find it difficult to open up and seek support following a major life adversity. One of the reasons for this relates to the 'MUM effect'. Based on research, psychologists have found that people are more reluctant to share bad news than good news. As a result, people do not talk about their issues to others. They bottle it up, leading them towards loneliness and isolation.

Gabbie loved everything about school: the learning, the friendships, the teachers, the feeling, the leadership, and even just walking in the playground.

During Year 11, before being diagnosed, Gabbie was given the privilege of being the Assistant Head Girl for Year 12. After being diagnosed, she became really worried that she was not going to be able to achieve her full potential in immersing herself in the leadership position, something she was passionate about and dreamt for many years.

Once it was time to step up and lead in Year 12, Gabbie had the full support of her senior leadership team, in particular Yasmine, the Head Girl. They shared the workload to allow Gabbie to fulfil her leadership duties in and around her studies and chemo treatment. Without their support, Gabbie would've burnt out.

Gabbie also faced the same challenges of performance-related stress, pressure and anxiety that other students faced on the journey through Year 12. However, it was through reaching out for the support of her family, friends and teachers that strengthened her to rise above her obstacles.

You do not have to lift the heavy weight of adversity alone. Just like the body builder, you can lift the weight with protection, guidance and support.

Who in your circle of support can you reach out to?
Your emotional muscle strengthens from finding courage to seek support, and also from the support you receive in the process.

THE FIGHTING SPIRIT

5, 6, 7, 8...

Two to go till ten, and the bodybuilder is in extreme pain and agony. His body is telling him to give up, but visions of his dream to become the bodybuilding champion flood his mind and give him further strength to keep going, along with the voice of his buddy pushing him to lift one more. It's at this greatest pain point where the greatest muscle growth is experienced. It's when it counts the most – the decision to persevere, to keep on going when feeling like giving up.

Gabbie experienced many physical, mental and emotional pain points.

In the first term of Year 12, Gabbie struggled to juggle her studies and the early stages of chemo treatment. She was constantly vomiting, had no energy and was unable to focus in class. There were times when she'd return home after school and just binge watch TV, feeling powerless and like she didn't care anymore.

When told that she would not receive her Higher School Certificate (HSC) because she'd be spending too much time in hospital and not in school, Gabbie could have easily accepted that as her fate and as an excuse to stop trying all together. Instead, she used it as motivation.

Rather than asking herself the question, 'Can I overcome this?', Gabbie instead focussed on answering the question, 'How can I overcome this?'

Despite struggling to cope early on, Gabbie's fighting spirit to persevere through her greatest pain points came from her family, who had every faith in her ability to overcome anything thrown at her. She didn't want to let them down.

Gabbie began tuning into what was not working for her and changed her approach so that she would not miss out on school. Each day, Gabbie prioritised improving her physical capabilities so she could attend school immediately after each chemo session to ensure she wasn't missing out on anything. Once at school, she would focus as much as she could in her classes for that day and upon returning home, she would sleep for three hours to recharge herself. This strategy worked well for her, as she stopped getting physically sick and feeling nauseated for the rest of her treatment, and was able to attend her classes.

By taking one day at a time and setting short term goals, it helped Gabbie stay on course. Upon achieving each small goal set, she received intrinsic reinforcement and belief to set and achieve the next goal, working her way towards achieving her overarching long term goal: to attend her graduation. It gave her something to aspire to and helped her in dealing with the side effects of chemo treatment.

When times got really tough, visualising herself on stage on graduation day, feeling proud, ignited hope and empowered her to take an extra step forward and persevere.

While there may be moments where the weight becomes so heavy you'll think about giving up, you'll be strengthened to persevere when there is *'faith, love* and *hope'* in your life (1 Corinthians 13:13).

For **faith**, seek inspiration from individuals who have been through what you're currently going through. They could be in your circle of support, or discovered from reading a book, watching a video, or hearing about them through another person. That dose of inspiration will give you the faith to persevere.

For **love**, think about your family and friends, and refer to moments in your life that you're grateful for. To any one of your family and friends, you are their world. How would your decision to persevere make an impact on them? What have they done for you that you can be grateful for to ignite the love to strengthen you to keep going for them?

For **hope**, remember, after every storm, there is a rainbow; after every night, there is light; and after every winter, there is spring. While pain is essential to building your emotional muscle, it does not last forever.

What can you look forward to after the storm? Before adversity struck, what were you excited about? What are your dreams and aspirations? Harness these visions and possibilities to provide you with a sense of purpose and another reason to believe and persevere. Tough times don't last but tough people do. Hope is found by never ever giving up.

> *For Gabbie, she found all three through her determination to win (faith), her family (love), and having something to look forward to by visualising her graduation day (hope).*

THE RIPPLE EFFECT

Just like a bodybuilder's muscles do not grow instantly after one workout, your emotional muscle won't grow overnight. It requires time and patience, but with winning emotions, protection and perseverance, your emotional muscle will grow, and in time you'll see the positive ripple effect of your choices.

Cancer could have easily been the perfect excuse for Gabbie not to attend classes, study, carry out her leadership duties, play netball, or stand out with optimism.

With cancer, as with any other type of adversity, you 'can-surrender' to it, 'can-survive' it, or you 'can-surpass' it and succeed. When told she only had a 20% chance of long-term survival, Gabbie was determined to overcome the insurmountable and believed she could surpass it and succeed.

After ninety-three chemotherapy sessions and twenty radiotherapy sessions, Gabbie not only finished her treatment a day before she turned eighteen, but also achieved outstanding results in her final Year 12 exams. This included defying the odds by only missing out on two weeks of school throughout the year.

She also emceed the Year 12 graduation ceremony, was awarded the school's most prestigious prize, helped fundraise $400,000 for charity to support other cancer patients, and was awarded Young Citizen of the Year, all within eighteen months after being diagnosed.

Gabbie's decision to build her emotional muscle and to never ever give up not only had a direct positive impact on her life and her family, but also created a positive ripple effect in others who were inspired by her story. It can certainly support those who are walking through the same journey she has walked.

In life, we cannot control the circumstances that are before us. The only thing we are in total control of is how we respond.

We become unstoppable by choosing to build the emotional muscle.

EXERCISE

Complete the following:

- Write down one simple gratitude exercise that you can do whenever you're feeling really down so you can change your state immediately from negative to positive and put things in perspective. It doesn't have to be time-consuming. It could be by just saying a positive phrase, listening to a song or through physical gestures, and it can be as short as ten seconds.

- Write down three things you can do to ensure faith, love and hope are alive and abundant in your life when times get tough. (Write one action for each.)

- In the face of adversity (whether currently experienced or yet to be experienced), you may feel like giving up. Visualise and describe the possible ripple effect of a decision to persevere through your greatest pain points.

SUMMARY

1. Adversity can strike at any time. You can cope and rise above challenges outside of your control by choosing to build your emotional muscle.

2. There are three stages to dealing with adversity – finding out, coming to terms with it, and taking control. The transition through each stage reveals a person's ability to recover effectively and build resilience.

3. Your emotional muscle will grow with winning emotions, protection and a fighting spirit, and with time, you will see the positive ripple effect of your choices.

11. IN CONTROL

"The secret to change is to focus all your energy not
on fighting the old, but on building the new."
— Socrates

When Bethany was seventeen, the death of her grandmother, the separation of her parents and the stress of her final year of school became all too much for her to handle. She struggled to get out of bed every morning for a prolonged period of time, feeling hopelessness and empty. She stopped doing the things she normally found enjoyable, like spending time with her dogs. When she began throwing and breaking things in the house out of anger and pain, she realised that she was struggling to cope. Bethany's mental health was not in good shape, and she was heading towards a downward spiral.

Just like how everyone has physical health, everyone has mental health. Physical injury is obvious but when it comes to mental health, it's not so obvious, but is just as important as physical health.

Mental health relates to the state of your mind – how you think, feel and act. Good mental health is when you can positively cope with the challenges and pressures of everyday life while still being able to live life to the fullest with a rich purpose, enjoyable experiences and meaningful relationships. When you do not look after your mental health, you'll struggle psychologically and emotionally with everyday challenges.

A mental health problem arises when there are significant changes in thoughts, feelings and behaviours that cause prolonged distress and interfere with daily functioning. When a mental health problem is left unmanaged and untreated, it can turn into a mental illness, just like how poor eating can lead to obesity and other physical illnesses.

There are different types of mental illnesses. The most common experienced by teens are anxiety, eating disorders and depression. Others types include Attention-Deficit-

Hyperactivity-Disorder (ADHD), bipolar disorders, addiction, and self-harm behaviour. These illnesses are usually interrelated and are caused by a variety of different factors.

Reaching out for support is difficult for most when experiencing a mental health problem. The three barriers that stop teens from seeking help are *fear*, *pride* and *blindness*.

Fear relates to being judged, not fitting in, being criticised and excluded, and being seen as 'different', 'weak' or as a 'wacko'. Fear leaves individuals not knowing who to speak to. Usually in denial, individuals filled with pride fear being judged and do not believe they could be affected by mental illness, and avoid seeking help when needed to show toughness.

Blindness relates to individuals who are not tuned in or aware of the onset of mental health problems. While ignorant in a way, they consider it part of growing up and not something serious enough that requires professional help.

Reaching out for help not only allows early intervention and treatment, but also enables you to maintain control of your life. It will empower you to see reaching out as vital, rather than shameful, and as a sign of strength, rather than weakness.

You'll discover that mental health problems are common and experienced by individuals from all walks of life, and not just the 'unlucky' few. You will also learn that the stigma and stereotypes connected to mental illness are not true, due to lack of education and exaggerations by media.

Seeking help is healing, and all thoughts, emotions and behaviours experienced till that point which did not make any sense to you at the time start to make sense. You will feel inner peace with acknowledgment and understanding, and you will find it easier to exercise the self-compassion required to accept where you are currently at. More importantly, you'll be encouraged by the opportunity to seek appropriate treatment.

> *Many celebrities who live with a mental illness – like Selena Gomez, Bruce Springsteen, Prince Harry and Amanda Seyfried – have voiced the importance of asking for help. In particular, Demi Lovato, who at eighteen was diagnosed with bipolar disorder, an incurable illness only manageable through regular treatment, has taken one step further by becoming a leading advocate with 'Be Vocal: Speak Up for Mental Health', an initiative encouraging people to use their voice in support of mental health.*

If you do not reach out for help, you'll continue to suffer in silence and potential illnesses will be left undiagnosed and untreated.

Research shows that teens who try to deal with mental health issues on their own are more likely to resort to harmful coping strategies like self-medicating with alcohol and drugs, over- or under-eating, and self-harming behaviour to numb internal pain. In this state, control is lost and feelings of hopelessness, loneliness and unworthiness emerge, increasing the risk of suicidal thoughts.

For the remaining parts of this chapter, I will share the three 'musts' when it comes to maintaining control in the face of a mental health problem and to effectively manage it.

In sharing these three 'musts', the **analogy of a ship sailing through sea** will be used. The ship represents your life, the weather and waves represents life situations and events, the sails represent your emotional and mental state, the destination represents your dreams and aspirations, the people on board represent your circle of support, and you are the captain of your ship.

1) DETECT THE UNUSUAL

While sailing your ship on the journey through life in the direction of your dreams, there may be times when you detect the unusual. The ship may have drifted in an unknown direction, perhaps caused by strong waves, strong winds and a change in weather. You're meant to be travelling north, but find yourself travelling east. The ship may be finding it difficult to function and navigate through the waters. As captain of your ship, the main thing is to detect the unusual and be aware that something is not right, even if you do not know what it is or what caused it.

At twenty-two, several years after completing high school and achieving outstanding results, Raj had a really tough year, experiencing a nasty end to a long-term relationship, as well as the passing of three family members - both grandparents and cousin. During this time, he was having abnormal mood swings and just wasn't feeling himself.

One day, a friend came to see him, and noticed something was not right. Taken aback, Raj became defensive and explained that he was "just busy". With caring intentions, his friend encouraged him to go see a doctor to make sure everything was ok.

At the time, Raj was a proud individual and didn't believe he had a problem, coping with issues by channelling his energy into work so he didn't think about them, unknowingly sabotaging himself from seeking help.

His initial thoughts about his situation was that he lacked essential vitamins and iron, so when he finally decided to get checked out by a doctor, he had no fear, mainly because he was unaware about mental health.

When diagnosed with a mental illness, Raj was super

apprehensive at first, mainly because he believed the diagnosis was indirectly labelling him as a loony. After calming down once the doctor explained his condition further, he not only gained a better understanding of it, but also realised that the mental health stigma that he had was false. Instead, it was just his ego talking.

Ditching his ego, he started exercising self-compassion and began appreciating his issue more, seeing it as something he can manage with the right support, rather than as an impediment.

It's easy to know when you've got a broken leg that you find it difficult to function daily. With mental health, it takes a greater awareness to know if you are effectively coping with the challenges of everyday life. It requires regular self-checkups measured over a period of time to detect and red flag the unusual, not based on just one bad day.

Here are five areas to monitor as part of your regular self-checkup:

1. **The wolf you're feeding.** Are your thoughts mainly positive or negative? Constant thoughts like 'What's the point?', 'I feel like giving up,' or 'I don't care' must be flagged as unusual.

2. **The way you're functioning.** This includes your energy levels, sleep patterns, concentration levels, eating patterns and breathing. Feeling always run down, lethargic and unfocussed are red flag signals.

3. **The way you're feeling.** Do you feel angry, overwhelmed, anxious, miserable or unhappy? When triggered occasionally, these emotions are normal. If they persist over time, they are red flags. For example, grieving the loss of a loved one is prolonged, igniting other unhealthy emotions that impact daily functioning.

4. **The way you're acting.** Thoughts create feelings that lead to certain behaviours or lack thereof. Examples include verbal and physical aggression, self-medicating with alcohol and drugs, compulsive acts, disengaging with and falling behind at school, and not doing the things that you'd normally find enjoyable. In Bethany's case, she detected the unusual when she stopped spending time with her animals and constantly released anger by breaking things.

5. **The way you're interacting with family and friends.** If you're spending less time with them, not going out as much, and prefer to keep to yourself, then this is a red flag.

All the above areas are interrelated, and, unless monitored, can create an unhealthy cycle of negativity.

The first step is to acknowledge that something is not right, even if you do not know what the issue is. You may feel that something is not right, or another person may detect it.

Go online and visit leading mental health websites (see resources) to understand the different causes of mental illness, as well as learning about the common signs of mental illness.

Do not feel ashamed or weird. It's the same thing as when you are feeling under the weather and looking up the symptoms of cold and flu.

Self-compassion is required to acknowledge that it is okay not to be okay, and when you accept rather than deny it, you'll find it easier to do something about it, rather than be held back by fear, pride or blindness.

2) SEND OUT AN SOS EARLY

SOS is an international code signal for extreme distress, and used frequently by ships at sea in trouble. When distressed by strong winds, waves, or a storm, sending out a SOS signal for help will not only prevent your ship from heading further into the wrong direction, but also strengthen your ability to withstand the tough conditions.

When her parents divorced while completing Year 12, Brenda found herself caught in the middle of a negative and toxic environment. In an attempt to cope, Brenda began drinking and taking drugs, not considering the physical risks and her own self-care.

Carrying lingering hurt and anger several years after her parents' divorce, Brenda reached a tipping point at twenty-five where it all became too much to handle, so she broke off her engagement to her fiancé at the time.

As painful as that decision was, it raised the need for Brenda to seek help after her prolonged depressive state was brought to light. Once she built up the courage to see a psychologist, she wished that she had reached out earlier, rather than trying to cope on her own.

In seeking help, she overcame her fears associated with being looked upon by others differently, discovering that her condition was more common than she thought. In turn, Brenda became more grateful for the things and for the people she did have in her life, rather than being pulled down by negative emotions.

With help, Brenda was able to exercise more patience and to become more deliberate with removing negative influences. She learnt to trust others, and set small short-term goals to move forward and build her confidence and self-image.

Once the unusual is detected, the thought of possibly having a mental health problem creates a natural human reaction of avoidance due to fear and pride. As soon as you become aware that something is not right, send an SOS out while you're still in control so things don't get worse. The longer you leave it, the worse it will get.

When determining who to speak to first from your circle of support, each person is different. There is 'no one size fits all'. Some people feel more comfortable opening up first to a family member, teacher or close friend; some prefer speaking to their school counsellor or local doctor, while others prefer using the free phone and online support available by leading mental health organisations.

Never assume others are too busy to help you, because you'll be surprised how supportive others are of someone in need. However, you need to let them know.

It's not always easy to start a conversation about mental health. Applying what was discussed in chapter 6, fear is a sound that you can reduce the volume to by increasing the sound of confidence with effective preparation.

Here are a few suggestions to build your confidence and courage to help you start the conversation with a friend or family member:

1. **Book it in**. Choose the most comfortable person you're willing to open up to. Arrange a day and time to catch up with them. At this point, keep it casual. Do not tell them the reason why.
2. **Have the conversation.** Allow for chit chat initially about general stuff to allow both of you to feel comfortable. Then, before you share your situation, ease into it by asking the following question very casually, "Do you know much about the topic of mental health and mental illness? It

keeps popping up at school and online." You'll be surprised given how common mental illness is today. If they respond with good knowledge of the subject, this is comforting because you'll know they'll be understanding when listening to your situation. They might even share a personal experience.

3. **Don't take it personally.** If they respond with something like, "Yeah, it's got to do with those psychopaths and loony people... ", it's because their response is based on lack of understanding and education. Stay calm and casually respond by drawing upon the comparison between physical health and mental health in simple terms, like I shared earlier. This will prepare them for what they will hear next.

4. **Ask questions.** Depending on how the conversation flows, you may want to ask further questions before opening up.

5. **Don't hold back.** When opening up, let it all out. Do it without fear.

6. **Take in feedback.** Once you've opened up, you'll earn great respect from showing courage. Allow them the opportunity to ask questions. It can be a huge shock in some instances. Take the opportunity to ask them if they detected anything unusual in the days and weeks leading up to the conversation, and for any suggestions relating to seeking professional help.

It's never easy before doing it, but you'll always feel glad once you've done it. It will help you realise that it wasn't that bad after all and that you are not alone. Once you've had the conversation, finding the right help will depend on your situation. Once again, there is 'no one size fits all'. Each person's needs are different. There are no magic pills.

It may take going through several health professionals before finding the right one, which takes time, so be patient. The benefit of seeing a professional is that they do not know anything about your past, which removes the fear of being judged. If you do not like your local doctor, because you do not feel comfortable or don't feel like you connect, don't allow that to stop you from seeking other health professionals. Seek until you find what's right for you. Positive influences and real-life stories will empower you along your journey.

3) ADJUST THE SAILS

While battling depression, Bethany was on the edge, cutting herself at times and feeling suicidal.

When Bethany opened up about her issues to her circle of friends and boyfriend, they were very supportive by being there when needed and having regular conversations to make sure she was okay. These positive relationships suppressed Bethany's suicidal thoughts, because deep down she didn't want to hurt those she loved by taking her own life.

Bethany loved animals and, before her depression, was passionate about pursuing a career in zoology. She believed deep down that it was her life purpose. After being disengaged during the core of her depression, Bethany, in taking one step forward, resumed spending time with her animals, lifting her up and reigniting that deep connection with them.

Regular counselling and a strong circle of support enabled Bethany to initially cope with depression, and it was through directing her energy to the things that brought her joy, purpose and hope, like animals, that enabled her to climb out of it.

> "A smooth sea never made a skillful sailor."
> — African Proverb

Life is unpredictable. Some things cannot be controlled, like the weather. By taking responsibility of your thoughts, feelings and behaviour, along with support and positive coping strategies, you can adjust the sails of your ship during the rough weather periods to redirect your life towards joy, purpose and abundance.

These self-care tips should help you adjust your sails when dealing with a mental health problem.

1. **Be alert**. Awareness of trigger points can help you keep your positive guard up when they do show up so you're prepared and unaffected, avoiding an unhealthy cycle of negativity.

2. **Be moving**. Your physical health directly affects the way you feel. Doing any form of exercise makes you feel good afterwards. Find what works for you and do it daily. Examples include walking the dog, sport, the gym, dancing, aerobics or riding.

3. **Be mindful**. Scientific research reveals that practicing mindfulness will allow you to be more present and relaxed, and will enable you to gain a greater understanding and control of your thoughts and feelings. Mindfulness will help you see that things aren't as bad as you may feel them to be, and it will show you the difference between what is in your control and what is not.

4. **Be in touch**. Other than professional support, remaining connected with family and friends continually will remove feelings of loneliness and helplessness, and bring joy and meaning into your life and remind you that you are not alone.

5. **Be thankful**. Exercise gratitude daily, as shared in the previous chapter, and you'll find that it'll always trump negative emotions. It will empower you to accept your challenges, rather than run from them.

6. **Be in love**. Love conquers all things so make time to do the things that bring joy, purpose and hope into your life. It could be music, art, sport, writing, dancing, shopping, going to the movies, community initiatives or helping the poor.

7. **Be patient**. Recovery takes some time, so take one day at a time. Set small goals daily to be your confidence boosters and these will elevate your mood. In no time, you'll be able to reflect on how far you've travelled, which will further encourage you. Always remember, things will always get better. No storm lasts forever.

From personal experience, I've found the above medication-free strategies to be very effective. You may discover a few of your own that make a positive difference and I encourage you to apply them with guidance from your support network. Your health professional will provide you with a treatment plan that is best for you based on your specific situation. If medication is required, usually for severe illnesses, this will be advised by your health professional.

Some mental illnesses can be fully recovered from, while others are incurable and only manageable through ongoing treatment, just like asthma and diabetes. While each case of mental illness varies, a great life can still be lived in spite of it.

LIFE IS NEVER SMOOTH SAILING

Just like for many, life was never smooth sailing on my journey towards achievement and living life to the fullest.

Since the 180-degree turning point where I excelled in Year 12, I went on to graduate from university, becoming a fully qualified Chartered Accountant at twenty-three, and worked in Australia's leading accounting firms in senior leadership roles throughout my twenties. As my journey continued through adulthood, I became a professional speaker and along the way travelled to twenty-five countries. The journey thus far has been a bumpy rollercoaster ride, with many highs and many lows, and I'm grateful for both.

But there came a point on the journey when life became too much to handle.

After months of sleepless nights, I knew something was not right. My anxiety levels were at an all-time high. I was less socially active than usual. I would have regular mood swings. Every morning was a mission to get out of bed. I was taking longer to process things, complete tasks and even communicate my thoughts, which increased my social anxiety. I was not being my usual self.

I had a basic understanding of mental illness but not enough for answers. When jumping online to research different types of mental illnesses, it felt uncomfortable at first, but then empowering. It changed my view on mental illness, enabling me to see how common it was amongst adults and teens and how far from the truth the stigmas were. While reading about the common signs of mental illness, I was able to connect some dots related to my personal situation and wanted to find out more.

Despite the fears, I opened up to my sister and then to my best friend in a very casual way and shared some of the things I was going through. Even though they knew me well, they didn't know the full story behind closed doors and beneath the surface, so it was a surprise to them at first.

As I was speaking, I felt the nerves in my voice, but the more I spoke, the more relieved I felt. They were non-judgmental, understanding, supportive and encouraged me to seek professional help.

Within a few days, I saw my local doctor, who then referred me to see a psychiatrist. I walked into his semi-dark room, sat down and waited for him to speak. He was gentle, of an Asian background and looked like a comedian if you asked me. He began asking me a series of questions, some more confronting than others. It was difficult at times to verbalise certain experiences that ran deep and dated back to childhood, but I felt strengthened with each word I said. I found it liberating sharing my experience when I was diagnosed at 13 with Attention Deficit Hyperactivity Disorder, and placed on medication. He made me feel really comfortable and we also shared a few laughs.

Once completed, I was diagnosed with an anxiety disorder called Obsessive Compulsive Disorder (OCD), an incurable mental illness only manageable through regular treatment.

While confronting my problem, I felt relieved when receiving the diagnosis because it provided an explanation to the many OCD-driven thoughts and behaviours experienced over the years.

Growing up and through adulthood, I would perform certain rituals daily like wetting my face frequently, excessively checking things like if the car door is locked or if the tap is turned off properly, and repeating things unnecessarily like washing hands.

At the time, I didn't understand why I was doing these things, but just accepted it. I didn't know I was living with an undiagnosed mental illness. When life became too much to handle and I had severe anxiety, the frequency of these thoughts and actions increased. It became physically and mentally draining, and it began to significantly interfere in my daily life, which prompted me to seek help.

It hasn't been an easy journey dealing with OCD, but with ongoing support and positive coping strategies, I've accepted that my illness is a lifelong management process and have not only learned to adjust my sails and live with it, but also to thrive in spite of it, not allowing it to define and stop me from living a happy, healthy and successful life.

ONE MORE

What do you do when you feel like you can't go any further, when you don't believe there is sunshine after the rain, when you feel like giving up?

When I was nineteen, a short time after finishing school, I received a phone call at 3am. It was from Melio, a close friend of mine. While Melio was living at home, Melio's stepfather was an alcoholic, and every night there would be an episode of verbal and, in some cases, physical abuse. Melio was also battling a severe mental illness.

When speaking on the phone, Melio's voice was light, but shaking. It took just hearing a few words to hear his indirect cry for help and to know that he was on edge and inches away from taking his own life.

I was the only person he felt he could talk to. I rushed over to his place, and just sat with him, not adding drama to an already dramatic situation. I approached the time with him like every other time we've hanged out – cracking a few jokes in between the serious talk to calm him.

If a stranger was looking over, they would never have suspected that Melio was on the edge, but by making the call in the dead of night, it was enough to enable him to have one more chat and to be reminded of how great he is, supported he is, and the possibilities that lie ahead. In hindsight, having one more chat when at his lowest gave Melio a lifeline and saved him from taking his own life.

When you feel at your lowest, like there is no hope, purpose or meaning to your life, remember that God has a purpose for you.

Time after time, an inspiring Bible verse that serves truth – personally and for others – during really low points is from Jeremiah 29:11, which goes, " 'For I know the plans I have for you' says the Lord. 'Plans to prosper you and not to harm you, plans to give you hope and a future.'"

It's not clear when you're at your lowest, but like many suicide survivors have discovered, time reveals this truth. Holding on for one more chat can make all the difference. It could be with a family member, relative, friend, teacher, coach, counsellor, youth worker, or with one of the 24/7 suicide prevention lines (see resources).

Always remember, just like the sun was made for light, you were born with a purpose, even when experiencing a mental health problem or living with a mental illness. Most importantly, you can still live a life of achievements and abundance when you learn how to adjust your sails.

EXERCISE

Complete the following:

- Conduct a self-checkup by reflecting upon the last six weeks and listing possible red flags. Where there are no red flags, schedule a self check-up at least once a month to monitor your mental health.
- Consider the three main barriers to seeking help – fear, pride and blindness – and describe your greatest barrier. Once identified, write down one thing you can do to break through this barrier.
- Using the suggestions earlier as guidance, create your own personalised approach to starting a conversation about your mental health with one trusted person from your circle of support.

  After you've had the conversation, immediately (within three days) schedule an appointment with your school counsellor or medical professional for professional support and guidance.

SUMMARY

1. While just as important as physical health, mental health relates to how you think, feel and act. When not looked after, it can lead to a mental health problem, and if left unmanaged and untreated, it can turn into a mental illness.

2. Three barriers that stop teens from seeking help are fear, pride and blindness. Reaching out for help allows early intervention and treatment. It's vital, not shameful, and is a sign of strength, not weakness. Mental health problems are common and experienced by individuals from all walks of life. The stigma and stereotypes connected to mental illness are not true, due to lack of education and exaggerations by media.

3. There are *three 'musts'* for maintaining control to effectively manage a mental health problem. First, detect the unusual through regular self checkups. Then, send an SOS early by starting the conversation with someone from your circle of support. Lastly, adjust your sails with positive coping strategies. When you feel like giving up, just hold on for one more chat. It can make all the difference.

12. FOOTPRINTS

"Our prime purpose in this life is to help others. And if
you can't help them, at least don't hurt them."
— Dalai Lama

A rron was six when his family decided to leave the city and move into a two-bedroom cottage in a small country town in Tasmania. It was meant to be just a temporary home, next door to a huge block of land where they planned to build their dream family home within a year. It turned out to be a ten-year wait.

On the eighth year, Arron's parents invested their entire savings into a business venture in an effort to turn their family dream into reality. On the tenth year, the family moved into their dream home, and at seventeen Arron finally had his own bedroom.

Within months after moving in, the economy experienced a major downturn and Arron's parents were forced to sell their dream home. Arron and his brother moved out on their own, and Arron's grandmother, who was like a second mother to him, passed away during that same time.

Arron's final three years of school went from bottom to top, then to rock bottom – an emotional rollercoaster.

Despite what was happening, Arron invested a great deal of time at school helping others with their personal issues by offering advice and support, something he became well known for amongst his peers. When with friends, he was a good listener and was deliberate in ensuring people felt comfortable enough around him to allow them to open up about their problems.

In particular, Arron lived near Jake and they caught the same bus to school together. Jake was a loud character, full of energy and had a big group of friends. Arron got to know Jake over many bus trips, hearing almost all of his problems before Arron shared any of his problems. As they spent more time together, Arron sensed that there was something beneath the surface that was bothering Jake.

One morning when heading to the bus stop to meet Jake, Arron felt something was not right. Jake's text messages seemed very odd. Instead, Arron walked straight to Jake's place, only to find him drunk and vomiting. It was the first time that Jake had drunk alcohol. Arron cleaned him up, calmed him down, and stayed with him till he became sober. When calling his parents, Arron, in good faith, didn't reveal the true reason why Jake vomited, on the condition that Jake would talk about his issues.

Once sober, Jake revealed that his reason for drinking alcohol was to try and cope with the stress at school and the pain from losing a close relative, and to also end the niggling temptation of never trying alcohol. Arron gave positive advice to Jake and also shared some of his issues to show that everybody has problems. With Arron's friendship and support, Jake left the drunken episode behind him and moved forward to do really well at school and continue on to graduate from university.

In helping others get the monkeys off their back, it not only made Arron feel better about himself with the knowledge that he was making a difference, but in doing so, it brought to light the reality that every person has their own issues that they are going through, which helped him remove the 'why me' train of thought.

In the first eleven chapters of this book, I provided you with strategies so you can get the monkeys off your back and live up to your full potential. With an attitude of gratitude, it's time now to take what you've learned and to go out and help others get the monkeys off their back through the spirit of giving, just like Arron.

To truly live is when you give to and help others; and if you can, then why not? Here's the thing: everyone can, because everyone has the freedom to choose.

For some teens, giving can become an escape from reality and an opportunity to stay out of trouble by channelling energy into a positive outlet. For others, they have an innate desire to lift up others and make a positive difference.

Helping others will give purpose, meaning and abundance in your life and allow you to regain humility, because you have shifted your attention from yourself to others, enabling you to show greater empathy and compassion. That feeling of making a difference to another person's life, no matter how small, will fill you with joy; and this joy can become a source of strength when you experience tough times.

With no strings attached, helping others will fill their lives with love, hope and inspiration, which can lead to new relationships, strengthening existing relationships, and in some cases can be the difference between life and death.

When you give, you're able to see life and the world around you with a different set of lenses. Life becomes much brighter. It feeds your spirit to give and make a positive difference because you acknowledge what you do have and what others do not.

You'll learn more about people, society and life than you would have otherwise. Along the way, you'll meet great people with big hearts, who can become positive role models and in some cases lifelong friends.

Research shows many examples of people who have made millions financially, achieved celebrity status, accumulated an abundance of materialistic possessions and who are successful but not fulfilled. The people who are fulfilled, with or without millions of dollars, are the ones who contribute and give to others. Success alone can leave people feeling empty and lost. Success coupled with significance is the ultimate prize, and significance comes through being selfless and giving to others.

Without the spirit of giving, negative emotions are easily retained, and life becomes empty, meaningless and dark. You'll never appreciate the beauty of what you do have, but also the power and influence within you to make a positive impact on another person's life.

Giving can be in words, in time, in donations and fundraising, and in acts of kindness.

Here are a few practical ways to help others get the monkeys off their back and leave your footprints in their hearts. Feel free to add your own.

- Start a **friendly conversation** with peers who might be alone by simply saying "Hey, dude, how are you doing?' The rest will take care of itself.
- Share **encouraging words** to at least one person a day.
- Be the person that someone **can lean on** in the face of adversity, such as death, illness or family breakdown. It could be for a sibling, relative or friend.
- Give a **handwritten note** to a teacher to show genuine appreciation for the work they do.
- **Stand up non-violently to bullying** and be there to comfort those bullied.
- **Take part** in anti-bullying and suicide prevention initiatives.
- Where possible, become involved with your **school's student representative council**.
- Take part in **school-run volunteering initiatives** like The Vinnies Appeal Sleepout. Each school is involved in different initiatives. When I was a student, I took part in Meals on Wheels, Christmas Lunch for the Poor, and Project Compassion through Caritas Australia.

- Take part in **community-run volunteering initiatives.** If you are unsure where to start, speak to your parents or school who can guide you. You can also go online and find out about initiatives through some of the leading charities like St Vincents De Paul Society, Red Cross or Mission Australia.

- If a person close to you is **struggling and on edge**, start a conversation with the intention to listen to them first, and then offer support. It's not easy to do this, and sometimes there's the fear of saying the wrong thing or making things worse. But by just being there for them without saying too much is enough to be comforting and in some cases even life-saving. It takes time, so be patient.

"We rise by lifting others."
— Robert Ingersoll

By helping others, you are helping yourself, and the value you receive from helping others usually outweighs the amount you give.

When choosing how to give and contribute, take into account not only your passions, interests and strengths, but also your personal experiences that others can learn from and be inspired by. You may be one person, but one action can lead to a positive ripple effect.

Again, I was too young to see it at seventeen, but looking back as I finish writing this book, Oprah's words ring true. Everything really does happen for a reason.

I'm grateful for the obstacles and challenges faced during both my teen and adult years, not only because they have strengthened me, but they also provided me with the opportunity to write this book to help others get the monkeys off their backs too and to leave my footprints.

All individuals whose stories have been included in this book have exercised the spirit of giving on their journey, and by choosing to be featured in this book, they leave their footprints too.

Every person is fighting their own battle and every person is writing their own story while learning from the stories of others.

As you continue your journey and write your story, I hope you have enjoyed reading this book and that you use it to get the monkeys off your back, while leaving your footprints in the hearts of many along the way.

EXERCISE

Complete the following:

- Consider the people you know (e.g. family, relatives, friends, peers, teammates). Identify one person who you know is currently struggling in some way (e.g. social exclusion, studies, personal issues, grieving). Describe how you could possibly support this person and the feelings you would like them to experience as a result.
- Using the suggestions shared earlier and your own, list three practical ways to exercise the spirit of giving in your life. Next to each, describe the impact that your actions will have on recipients.
- List three ways in which your passions, strengths and personal experiences can be used for the benefit of others with no return to you.

SUMMARY

1. Helping others rewards you with abundance, meaning and purpose in your life. The value you receive from helping others is usually greater than the amount you give.

2. You have so much to offer and give to the world. Consider your strengths and passions as well as personal experiences that others can learn from and be inspired by when choosing how to help others.

3. Take what you've learned through reading this book to help others get the monkeys off their backs to leave your footprints in their hearts.

AFTERWORD

C ongratulations! You have reached the part of the book that most people will never reach.

This is not the end, though; it's just the beginning of your journey for igniting personal change so you can get the monkeys off your back and live up to your full potential.

By reading this book, you have demonstrated the hunger, initiative and commitment to grow and build your resilience in school and in life.

Now, it's time to take control by taking action.

"To know and not to do is not yet to know."
— Stephen Covey

When no action is taken, this book has little benefit.

Here are some important items to continue on your journey:

- Ensure you have completed all exercises. If you haven't, go back. Start from chapter one and complete one chapter per week. It's easy to get distracted, so it's important to block out the time and make it a priority.

- Set time aside and open up discussions with a trusted adult to gain further perspective and guidance about the things you've learned and discovered from reading this book. Share the responses to the exercises and seek feedback.

- Once you have completed the above, follow through and take action. I would recommend revisiting chapter five ('Winning Ingredients') to guide you with setting goals, and creating a plan that will work for you and that you will stick to. Remember to stay connected and be in regular contact with your trusted adult to monitor your progress.

Some messages become relevant over time and through experience, so I would recommend re-reading the book to take in what was missed the first time.

Feel free to email me directly if you have any specific questions or would just like to share your story. You can also connect with me on social media and subscribe to my YouTube channel.

Once again, congratulations on stepping into the driver's seat of your life. I'm very proud of you and look forward to hearing about your journey and the changes you've experienced from taking action after reading this book.

Please share with family, friends, parents, teachers, and anyone else who can benefit.

And lastly, be fearless in the pursuit that sets your heart on fire.

The best is yet to come.

On the following page, I leave you with my own **resilience creed**. It's a daily declaration and commitment, and one that I live by. I invite you to say this creed out loud with power and conviction every day as you walk the journey ahead.

THE RESILIENCE CREED

Today I decide,
To step up and take control,
To take full responsibility,
To be the leader of my life.
Today I decide,
To believe not doubt.
I am capable and worthy,
I can do anything I put my mind to,
I have unlimited potential,
I am like no other: one of a kind.
Today I decide,
To always embrace life's challenges,
For without them, I will not grow.
To always get back up and move forward,
To never ever give up.
Today I decide,
To get the monkeys off my back,
To live up to my full potential.
I have everything I need:
I have abundance around me,
I have the power within me.
With belief, all things are possible;
With drive, I am unstoppable;
With gratitude, I am unbreakable.
IT'S MY LIFE
I AM RESPONSIBLE (x 3)
This I decide, today, and every day I rise.

ADDITIONAL SUPPORT

I've endeavoured to provide you with as much guidance and support as possible, but there are some situations where it may not be enough, and could require you to seek further support that is tailored to your specific situation and needs.

Below is a list of Australian-based support services I strongly recommend reaching out to if you find yourself not in control and struggling to cope.

If you live outside of Australia, reach out to the equivalent in your country, starting with a simple Google search.

PHONE, WEBCHAT AND EMAIL

- **Beyond Blue** | 1300 22 46 36 | youthbeyondblue. com
  Free, private and confidential 24/7 counselling service for people of all ages.

- **Lifeline** | 13 11 14 | lifeline.org.au
  Free, private and confidential 24/7 counselling service for people of all ages.

- **Kids Helpline** | 1800 55 1800 | kidshelpline.com. au/teens

  Free, private and confidential 24/7 counselling service for young people aged between five – twenty-five years old.

  International equivalent: childhelplineinternational.org

- **Suicide Call Back Service** | 1300 659 467 | suicidecallbackservice.org.au

  Free, private and confidential 24/7 counselling service for anyone feeling suicidal, or anyone who knows another person who is feeling suicidal.

- **eheadspace** | 1800 650 890

  Free, private and confidential counselling service for young people aged between twelve–twenty-five years old to speak with a qualified youth mental health professional. Offered seven days a week from 9am – 1am AEDST (Australian Eastern Standard Time).

- **Emergency** | 000

FACE-TO-FACE

Health Professionals
First, your local doctor, who can then refer you to mental health specialists. Note: Australia's healthcare scheme is government-funded, and gives all citizens access to a wide range of health services at little to no cost. A Medicare card is required to access benefits. Once teens reach fifteen, they are eligible to receive their own card to be used when seeing health professionals, with all information relating to medical service usage kept confidential, even inaccessible by parents.

Headspace | headspace.org.au
Headspace centres are located across Australia where people can access health workers such as GPs, psychologists, social workers, alcohol and drug workers, counsellors, vocational workers or youth workers. Services are either free or at low cost.

RESOURCES

HELPFUL WEBSITES

The following are trusted and reputable websites that will save you time in accessing reliable information:

- **Reach Out** | au.reachout.com
  Practical support in the form of factsheets, stories, videos, information, tools and forums to help young people deal with life's challenges.

- **Bullying No Way** | bullyingnoway.gov.au
  The Australian government's anti-bullying website, with hints and tips on how to deal with verbal, physical and cyber bullying, and valuable information supporting all parties affected by bullying – the bullied, the bully, bystanders, parents, teachers and friends.

- **Bite Back** | biteback.org.au
  An interactive platform with a variety of activities, stories, interviews and blogs for young people to build their mental fitness – an initiative by the Black Dog Institute for 12 – 18 year olds.

- **Youth Beyond Blue | <u>youthbeyondblue.com</u>**
  Provides valuable information and support to help young people and their family and friends to detect and respond to anxiety and depression.

SMARTPHONE APPLICATIONS

For iOS only

- **My Gratitude Journal:** an easy way to enter into strong state of positivity in just five minutes.

For iOS and Android

- **Mental Stillness:** for guided meditation
- **Smiling Mind:** for guided meditation
- **Pacifica:** daily tool for managing stress, anxiety and depression
- **Moment:** for tracking your daily iPhone or iPad usage
- **Happify:** fun and interactive games and exercises to overcome negative thoughts and build resilience
- **Remente:** helps you set goals, increase motivation and reduce stress
- **Headspace**: for guided meditation
- **The 7-minute workout:** simple exercises that can be done anytime, anywhere to enhance your mood, release stress and make you feel awesome.
- **Self Control:** a free Mac application that helps you avoid distracting websites.

COMPUTER APPLICATIONS

- **Cold Turkey (Mac and Windows):** allows you to temporarily block distractions to get work done.
- **Self Control (Mac only):** helps you avoid distracting websites by temporarily blocking them.

ABOUT THE AUTHOR

Born to immigrant working-class parents, Daniel grew up in the southwestern suburbs of Sydney.

When he was one, he was placed in intensive care. Because of his severe asthma condition, the head doctor informed his parents that he wouldn't make it.

Having escaped possible death, Daniel faced many challenges growing up. Bullied for a decade, diagnosed with a mental illness at thirteen, and labelled as a student with 'no hope,' Daniel's story is one of resilience. At sixteen, he turned his life around by breaking through personal, academic and social barriers to be listed in the Top 10% of Australia in academic achievement in Year 12.

At twenty-one, Daniel graduated with a Bachelor of Commerce (Professional Accounting) from Macquarie University, and by twenty-three became a fully qualified Chartered Accountant (CA).

While on a journey of self-discovery during his mid twenties, Daniel developed a passion for events, entertainment and public speaking. Armed with just a dream and burning desire, Daniel decided to step into unknown territory to become a professional Master of Ceremonies (MC), despite having never spoken in public.

Fearless in his pursuit, Daniel quickly built a name for himself, hosting events such as weddings, gala balls, charity events, beauty pageants, business seminars, product launches and outdoor festivals.

The highlight event of his career to date was hosting New Year's Eve on the Cahill Expressway 2017, which had a combined total of approximately 7000 people, with the best view of the Sydney Harbour Bridge and Opera House for the stunning fireworks display. Daniel is now considered one of Australia's leading MCs.

Despite his achievements in wearing the CA and MC caps, Daniel knew deep down that his life carried a much greater purpose and wanted to use his voice to help others. As a result, Daniel entered the inspirational speaking space, where he delivers messages of resilience to both youth and corporate audiences.

Having spoken and inspired thousands of people, Daniel's core message is to 'get the monkeys off your back', and is passionate about helping others break through their barriers so they can live up to their full potential. Any listener with ambition and drive will be motivated, empowered and inspired after hearing Daniel.

In March 2018, Daniel was awarded the prestigious Kerrie Nairn Scholarship by Professional Speakers Australia. The scholarship is awarded to assist the development of an emerging speaker to become an outstanding professional leader.

Through his speaking, writing and mentoring initiatives, Daniel hopes to create a multi-generational movement of resilient teens, believing the youth of today and tomorrow hold the key to making and shaping a brighter future for all.

Contact Information

- daniel@danielmerza.com
- www.danielmerza.com

SPEAKER BIO

One of Australia's most dynamic and engaging speakers, Daniel delivers high energy 'resilience-focussed' presentations to youth and corporate audiences.

Daniel has spoken to and inspired thousands of people, and is passionate about helping individuals break through their barriers and build resilience to overcome challenges so they can live up to their full potential.

Whether speaking to a high school, corporate, conference, or community audience, Daniel's presentations are impactful and transformational because he ensures his content and delivery are relevant, customised and tailored to the audience he is speaking to, so they can walk away empowered to take immediate action.

A **resilience expert**, Daniel's presentations cover the following:

- Emotional intelligence
- Leadership and character development
- Overcoming fear
- Self-discovery
- School, career and life choices
- Mental health
- Bullying
- Social media addiction
- Peak performance

For more information about Daniel's motivational keynote presentations, workshops, seminars and mentoring programs, visit www.danielmerza.com.

If you would like to invite Daniel to speak at your school or organisation, you can send your enquiry through to enquiries@danielmerza.com with the subject line: Speaking Request.

LEAVE YOUR FOOTPRINTS

A story is worthless if remained untold.

Do you have a story of overcoming obstacles, hurdles and trials that demonstrates resilience and can inspire others on their journey?

Like myself and the individuals featured in this book, you can leave your footprints too by emailing your story to stories@danielmerza.com. You can share your journey and experiences, the key lessons you gained along the way, and the strategies you applied that enabled you to build your resilience, so that you can help others who may be on a similar journey.

These stories may be published on my website, social media, article, blog or included in another book to be written in the future. Prior to doing so, your consent will be obtained and you will have the option to keep your identity anonymous for privacy purposes.

I look forward to reading your story, and I hope you can join me on the journey to create a multi-generational movement of resilient teens.

Daniel Merza

Printed in the USA
CPSIA information can be obtained
at www.ICGtesting.com
LVHW041803211123
764514LV00006B/175